D0649533

STONYHURST SCRIPTURE MANUALS

THE
GOSPEL ACCORDING
TO SAINT MARK

With an Introduction and Commentary

by

C. C. MARTINDALE, S.J.

THE NEWMAN PRESS
WESTMINSTER, MARYLAND
1956

First published in U.S.A., 1956

Imprimi Potest
>J. D. Boyle, S.J.
>Praep. Prov. Ang. Soc. Jesu.

Nihil Obstat
>Sebastian Bullough, O.P., S.T.L.

Imprimatur
>✠ Josephus
>>Epis. Cliftoniensis.

15 June, 1955.

PRINTED IN THE UNITED STATES OF AMERICA

EDITORIAL NOTE

STONYHURST Scripture Manuals fill many of the needs satisfied fifty years ago by the Manuals of Father Sydney Smith, S.J., of *The Month* staff. These earlier works are now out of print and, in any case, unsuited to present needs.

The commentary and notes are the work of Father C. C. Martindale, who has a long-standing reputation for Biblical scholarship. In order to pass on the benefit of his knowledge to the beginner, he has worked throughout in collaboration with members of the Stonyhurst staff who have many years of experience in teaching Scripture.

Any individual or group engaged in studying the New Testament will find in this and successive volumes the means of deepening their knowledge of the life and Person of Christ, and so of coming to a truer and more intimate understanding of Him.

PHILIP CARAMAN, S.J.

GENERAL INTRODUCTION

THIS series is intended for the use of schools, especially for those who enter for public examination, and therefore the version called the 'Douay' has throughout been quoted, despite the imperfections whether of the English translation or the Latin original. The notes have been kept as short as possible: we have not made use of devotional comments or applications, nor, save by exception, strictly theological ones. On the other hand, we have tried to include what might throw light on the conditions in which our Lord lived and spoke. It would be impossible to catalogue the authorities that we have used: happily we can now refer to the *Catholic Commentary on Holy Scripture* (1953): besides, we have the Westminster Version with its notes, and the books by the late Fr Hugh Pope, O.P., and the monumental volumes produced by the late Fr M.-J. Lagrange, O.P., our debt to whom we never can repay.

A practical difficulty remains. The books on the Synoptists are produced separately, so that there cannot but be many repetitions unless teacher or pupil have all three at hand and are ready to refer constantly from one to the other. Pupils, at least, are not likely to do this: therefore the repetitions cannot be avoided, though the difficulty of 'harmonization' will not always be surmounted. But the *Commentary* alluded to above should give the teacher all he needs to know. We pray that the study of the Gospel may become always more intelligent as well as more spiritual.

The inclusion of a certain number of Greek words should not deter boys or schools who do not take that language. They are always given with the (Douay) English; and are quoted because the English often does not and sometimes cannot render the full flavour of the Greek. Besides, some Greek words may be used chiefly, or only, by the author in question, and 'characterize' him, and he ought to be given his chance of 'coming to life', even though the English equivalents may be, at best, very imperfect.

INTRODUCTION TO SAINT MARK

I Preliminary

THE Christian Church existed before the 'gospels' and produced them. What do they profess to be? Not 'Lives' of our Lord, but records of His *Message*. They were 'the Good News'. The document written by St John stands alone: the writings of St Matthew, St Mark and St Luke provide a problem, because they both differ among themselves and are also like one another, and even coincide, word for word, with one another. How did this come about? There was, we know, a *spoken tradition*, that is, a doctrine officially taught and probably partially learnt by heart, as Jewish children learnt much of the Old Testament and as Mohammedan children still learn much of the Koran. But besides this, there were documents which contained this teaching in writing; and St Luke, who composed his 'gospel' about 59 or 60 (see Introduction to Luke), says that 'many' such documents were already in circulation. By 'many' he cannot have meant *only* Matthew and Mark. The authors of these documents proposed to give an account of 'the things that have been accomplished amongst us, according to what those who were eye-witnesses from the beginning . . . handed down to us'; therefore, 'I too', says St Luke, 'who have from the outset accurately followed up everything, decided to write it down in order, for you, noble Theophilus, that you may thoroughly understand the solid truth of the teaching that you have received (κατηχήθης: the *catechesis* of which you were the 'catechumen')'. It is clear then that Theophilus, to whom St Luke dedicates his treatise, had received oral instruction in the Faith and its historical origin (acts, or events, πράγματα);

and that several written accounts of this were accessible, and that Luke examines these and compiles his 'gospel' from those he considers the most reliable. Therefore, since no trace survives of any document earlier than those by Matthew and Mark, since Luke often coincides with one or both of these, we have to ask what was the relation between them. He certainly did not merely copy either (for he adds much material found in neither of them and often rearranges what he does take over), nor did any of the three merely repeat one 'oral tradition'; and yet, the verbal coincidences in all three are often so striking that we are driven to admit they all followed a 'central' oral tradition, so to say, and each, very likely, read the other two but none the less pursued his own method of telling his story. Since this volume, however, is about St Mark, and since no one thinks that Matthew or Mark borrowed from Luke, we have only to ask what was the relationship between Mark and Matthew. The tradition in the early Church is solid—St Matthew wrote first. Coincidences must then be due to Mark's copying Matthew where both do not depend on the oral tradition or some independent source. But nowadays it has been the habit to argue that St Mark wrote first. The real reason for this is that St Mark says nothing about the miraculous Birth of our Lord, and very little about the Resurrection, so it becomes easier to say that the narratives in Matthew (and Luke) are later mythical additions. There is no evidence at all for this. It is true that St Matthew wrote his gospel, to begin with, in Hebrew or Aramaic; this was afterwards translated into Greek by himself or another, and the translator *may* have known St Mark. Anyway, we have no reason to suppose that the Greek 'Matthew' differed in any substantial way from the Hebrew or Aramaic original.

We must again recall that the 'gospels' are not 'Lives of Christ', but put into writing such parts of His doctrine as were preserved by the Church and handed down together with significant actions of His which threw light upon that doctrine. Inevitably each writer would make his own sort of record. Divine inspiration does not alter a man's vocabulary, his syntax, his favourite turns of phrase, his literary 'style' and method. You must distinguish between what he means to say, and his way of saying it. St Mark will remain relatively rough; St Luke more polished. This makes the verbal coincidences between the 'Synoptists' often quite startling. It accounts, too, for many of their differences—thus one Evangelist may write down a saying of our Lord's out of its proper place, because something he has just written has reminded him of it; and he may put it in his own words, not quite as the other Evangelists do. In fact, exact quotation is a fairly modern practice; all the Evangelists mention the Title over the Cross—which was short and easily memorized—yet none of them refers to it in quite the same words. Neither do we know the exact words of the Institution of the Holy Eucharist. When our Lord makes use of the Old Testament, He adapts it, rather than quotes it verbally. All the more striking is it that the Gospels give us so harmonious and so living a portrait of our Lord. No ancient literature that we know of presents so perfect a picture of anyone. Either their descriptions are dead, or modified by political or personal prejudices, or as different as the accounts of Socrates given by Plato, Aristophanes and Xenophon.

In the following Notes we propose to indicate the more important coincidences, or divergencies, to be observed in the three Synoptists, only occasionally alluding to John.

II SAINT MARK AS AUTHOR

The second document in our New Testament is called 'The Gospel according to Saint Mark'. When St Peter escaped from prison, he went (Acts 12: 12) to the house of Mary, mother of 'John surnamed Mark': when Barnabas and Saul left Jerusalem for Antioch and then started on the 'first missionary journey' they took with them Barnabas's young kinsman,

'John surnamed Mark' (12: 25, and see Col. 4: 10): they went first to Barnabas's home-land, Cyprus, and crossed to Pamphylia, but here 'John' left them (Acts 13: 13)—why, we do not know, but Paul (as he now named himself) must have thought him unreliable, for when Barnabas proposed to take 'John called Mark' with St Paul on a later journey, St Paul refused; a sharp dissension took place between Barnabas and Paul, and the former carried St Mark off with him to Cyprus (Acts 15: 7–39). This event occurred about A.D. 52, but friendly relations must have been re-established well before 62, since Paul, writing from Rome to the Colossians (Col. 4: 10), salutes them in his own name and that of 'Mark, kinsman of Barnabas', adding: 'about whom you have been bidden to welcome him, should he arrive among you': to Philemon (24) he writes of St Mark and others as his fellow-workers: and again (2 Tim. 4: 11): 'Take Mark and bring him with you, for he is very useful to me for the ministry.' Finally, St Peter (1 Peter 5: 13) writes: 'The Church in Babylon [i.e. Rome] salutes you, and so does Mark, my son.' St Peter was martyred, we hold, in A.D. 64: St Paul, in 67 or 68.

The oldest and most important witness to St Mark's authorship is that of Papias, bishop of Hierapolis, quoted in Eusebius's *History of the Church*, III, xxxix, 15. Papias wrote about A.D. 125, and is reporting what 'the Presbyter John' stated (it is disputed whether this Presbyter was the Apostle himself, or a prelate in close touch with him and able to consult him on important matters). Papias wrote: 'And this the Presbyter used to say: "Mark was the 'interpreter' of Peter, and wrote down all that he remembered (or, 'that Peter called to attention') what had been said or done by the Lord—accurately, but in no (systematic) order." For he had neither listened to the Lord nor followed along with Him, but afterwards, as I said, (went with) Peter. He (Peter) used to give his instructions according as need arose, but not as proposing to make an orderly arrangement of the Lord's words. So Mark was not at fault, because he wrote down thus certain things according as he remembered them. He was concerned only with this—to omit nothing that he had heard, and not to set down anything of it untruthfully.' It is much more probable that Papias quotes the Presbyter only up to the words 'systematic order', and that what follows is his own comment, ἔφην being 'as *I* said', and not 'as he (the Presbyter) said'.

The tradition that St Mark founded the Church in Alexandria and was bishop there is not known before A.D. 200, but no alternative career is spoken of. One old writer says he was κολυβοδάκτυλος, i.e. had stumpy fingers, rather than that he had amputated, e.g., a thumb to escape from the Jewish priesthood towards which he had been urged.

The point is, that St Mark put into writing what St Peter taught by word of mouth: Mark was nearly what we would call Peter's 'secretary', and had seemingly been criticized for writing down just what Peter said as occasion demanded it, instead of grouping doctrine and events—e.g. parables or miracles—as Matthew had done. For our purposes it seems unnecessary to quote all the ancient authorities who tell us that Mark put Peter's verbal teaching (*catechesis*) into writing. St Justin, writing in Rome about 150, does not mention Mark by name, but does speak of the 'Memoirs of Peter' and quotes the giving of the 'nickname' Boanerges to James and John which is recorded only in Mark. St Irenaeus (d. 202) says that after the death of Saints Peter and Paul 'Mark, Peter's disciple and interpreter, himself also left us in writing the preaching of Peter'. It is true that Clement of Alexandria (d. c. 215) says that many asked Mark to write down what Peter had said, and that when St Peter heard that this was being done he neither approved nor disapproved. But we think it probable, and in keeping with Peter's humility, that Mark did indeed write down Peter's teaching while the Apostle was still alive, but gave, or lent, what he wrote only to those who asked for it; he did not *publish* it till after Peter's death (64).

But the date of St Mark's actual writing can probably be defined more closely. It is agreed that St Mark wrote before St Luke. But St Luke wrote the *Acts* towards the end of St Paul's first captivity in Rome (c. 63) and *after* his Gospel. We can, then, assume that St Mark wrote between 55 and 60, if not earlier, and that he wrote for Roman Christians, chiefly, not Jews. Given the shortness of St Mark's gospel, the amount of Latin words used is very high; e.g. *legio*, *speculator*, *denarius*, *sextarius*, *centurio*; and in 12: 42, the Greek word *lepton*, the smallest coin in use, is translated into *quadrans*, the smallest Latin coin, which we have in our turn to translate 'farthing'. Jewish customs are explained and Aramaic words translated (e.g. 7: 3; 3: 17; 5: 41; 7: 11, 34, etc.), and it would have been unnecessary to inform a Jew that the Jordan was a river (1: 5), or that the Mount of Olives was opposite the Temple (13: 3) or that the Parasceve was the day before the Sabbath (15: 42). On the other hand, there is very little about what was so important for Jews, e.g. prophecy, or about the preservation of the Mosaic Law even though Christ 'fulfilled' it. Finally, in 15: 20, Simon of Cyrene is casually mentioned as father of Alexander and Rufus, as though St Mark's readers would naturally recognize these names, and a 'Rufus' is saluted by St Paul when writing to Rome (Rom. 16: 13)

It is often argued that the comparative frequency with which St Peter is mentioned in Mark is in favour of the gospel having been written by someone closely in touch with him, while on the other hand he is *not* mentioned on occasions which might have redounded to his honour (e.g. Matt. 14: 29; 16: 18; 17: 24), and this is explained by his modesty and perhaps by an abiding sorrow for his denial of his Lord. More cogent, we think, are the many touches which suggest an eye-witness or at least a writer who was in close touch with one. Thus, in the boat our Lord sleeps with his head 'on *the* pillow' (4: 38): the men about to be fed sat down 'on the green grass . . . by fifties and hundreds' (6: 39, 40): the paralytic in 2: 3 was 'carried by four': 7: 32–37 contains a cure for blindness vividly told by St Mark and by him only. We can however get closer to the nature of St Mark's document. First, it was *written* by *one man*, even though it consists of what others, St Peter in particular, remembered.

It contains 7 words found nowhere else: but all these (save ἔννυχα, 'still dark' and κεφαλιοῦν, 'beat over the head', which may well be words in popular use) consist of the addition of a preposition to an ordinary word (e.g. ὑπερ-ἐκ-περισσῶς 'very, very much'). However, there are many words that he *likes*, which appear in his short gospel more often than in Matthew or Luke: e.g. ἔρχεται(-ονται), 'He (they) comes (come)'; Mark, 25 times; Matt, 3 times; Luke, 1. εὐθύς (immediately), Mark 42; Matt. 18; Luke 7. περιβλέπομαι (I look around at), Mark 6; Luke 1. πολλά (much) used adverbially: Mark, 9 times; Paul, 4. ἤρξατο(-αντο), 'he, they, began', Mark 26; Matt. 9; Luke 19. Mark constantly uses καί 'and' instead of δέ (practically 'and'): he uses δέ 156 times; Matt., 496; Luke, 508: had Mark's brief document used it in the same proportion as the others, it should have appeared about 300 times. These peculiarities are distributed throughout 'Mark' and are not found in any special 'patch'.

St Mark is very fond of the historical present: 151 instances could be quoted; of these only 72 are the verbs λέγει; λέγουσι, 'he says, they say'; Matt. 78, of which 59 occur with that verb, and 15 in parables where Mark does not use it. Luke has only 4 or 6 instances and 5 in the parables. Mark's instances are, again, distributed throughout his work. He is fond too of *asyndeton*, i.e. lack of connecting particles, especially when our Lord's words are quoted, where Matthew or Luke insert δέ, καί, γάρ, οὖν. This makes for swiftness, and shows our Lord's *imperatoria brevitas*: e.g. 5: 39; 10: 14; 12: 27; 13: 7; 14: especially 12: 27: πολύ πλανᾶσθε: 'You are *quite* wrong'. Classical Greek loves a smooth and logical linking of its phrases: thus, 'therefore', appears about 200 times in John; 57 in Matthew; 31 in Luke; 3 in Mark.

Finally, Mark, though normally terse, often uses *pleonasms*, i.e. puts two words where one would suffice: a few instances only need be quoted: 4: 5: 'stony land where they had not much earth'; 9: 2, 'by themselves alone'; 14: 61, 'he kept silence and answered nothing': but often the second word reinforces and animates the idea and its expression: 5. 23: ἵνα ζωθῇ καὶ ζήσῃ 'be cured and live': The words merely mean 'cured', not 'live', i.e. spiritually, as they would in John. All recognize St Mark's vivid and concrete way of describing scenes—his affection for definite numbers: *four* men carry the paralytic (2: 3): the 2,000 swine (5: 13; cf. 6: 37; 4: 14: 5, etc.). A more consciously 'literary' Greek writer would have minimized his use of names of places, persons, hours, or of numbers, which is markedly what Luke does. And yet, Mark has only a few *forms* at his disposal, and is an inexperienced writer, slipping into his stereotyped phrases unconsciously. Space forbids long quotations: but compare the cure of the deaf and 'dumb' man (7: 32–36) with that of the blind man (8: 22–26): two accounts of our Lord's preaching (1: 21–27 and 6: 1–2): and 11: 1–6 with 14: 13–16. Mark's vivacity coupled with his literary poverty is but the more striking. We could not discuss here whether or no Mark's Greek is nearer to Aramaic (the language spoken by our Lord) than Matthew's or Luke's; but there is no reason to suppose that Mark's gospel was originally written in Aramaic, still less that it was written first in Latin. But it does suggest that its author was a strong personality, who wrote a popular Greek, while still thinking in Aramaic forms, and sufficiently familiar with the Roman world.

In old days, 'lives' of outstanding men were written, following them from birth to death, drawing morals (as Plutarch was soon to do) from their good or bad behaviour, or collecting a number of anecdotes about them (as Suetonius would do), or defending their subject against criticisms and pulling the evidence to their side, so that you had a picture rather of what the biographer thought, liked, and was, than of his subject. Not till modern times have biographers tried to 'analyse' the inner life, the gradual development, in short, the 'psychology' of their subject. But, we repeat, St Mark is not writing a biography. He is putting into writing a message—an *incarnate* message, no doubt; but he excludes our Lord's childhood and merely indicates His resurrection.[1] He does not seek to 'prove' that Jesus was the Messias: he does not argue (as St Matthew, writing for Jews, did) that prophecy was fulfilled in him: he quotes prophecy (1: 2; 9: 12 ff.) only about the Baptist: he shows our Lord consistently *not* using His miracles as public signs of Messiah-ship: there are no hints at all that His consciousness of that Messiah-ship developed: so honest is Mark that he does not shirk repeating what might seem a 'difficulty' in the way of admitting His divine nature— enough to mention His rejection of the name 'good' (10: 18): His assertion that not even the Son knows the hour of the Judgment (12: 32): His cry of desolation on the cross (15: 34). Where you do see 'development' is in the attitude of Scribes and Pharisees who gradually become clear that Jesus is a 'heretic' and must be got rid of. And if there is a 'turning-point' in His ministry, it is the Confession of St Peter, after which He devotes Himself almost wholly to the instruction of the Twelve. A modern historian might regret that St Mark did not insert our Lord's life and activities into the general history of His times; but He preached in Palestine, and St Mark's picture of that country and its customs is fully 'alive' and even picturesque: that he did not put his account of events into a rigidly chronological order was recognized and explained from the outset (Papias) and here and there his data are rearranged by St Luke and maybe St John; but sometimes St Mark does 'group' similar events or sayings together—the five conflicts with the Pharisees are placed together (2: 1–3: 6); and so are the parables of the Kingdom (4). In short, St Mark wrote with perfect integrity the sort of history he meant to write, 'leaving out nothing that he had heard and falsifying none of it'.

[1] We recall the history of Elias (3 Kings, 17 to 4 Kings, 2, 12).

III Saint Mark's Doctrine

No Jew needed to be taught that GOD exists, is eternal, all-powerful, and so exalted that His very Name must not be mentioned—the 'Heavens', the 'Power', and so forth were substituted for it. But the Jews thought of their history as one of election and vocation, of divine promises and revelations made to the Patriarchs and Prophets; and they looked forward to the Kingdom of God—the Triumph of God upon earth, due to the 'conversion of hearts', and, sometimes, proclaimed by a miraculous intervention from on high. But by many, this prospect was interpreted materialistically—a King should arrive, evicting all pagans from Palestine, and reigning in splendour at Jerusalem. Our Lord did not scorn these ideals, but began *where His hearers were*, speaking 'according as they could understand' (4: 33) and gently leading them to more spiritual thoughts about both Kingdom and King.

'The time is full-filled: the Kingdom of God has drawn near' (1: 15): but the parables of the seed and the mustard-tree (4: 26: 30) show that the realization of the Kingdom-on-earth would be gradual: the meaning of His parables was not obvious but a 'mystery', explained at first in private to the Twelve (4: 11): the Kingdom must be entered into here at heavy cost (9: 47 ff.) but its full enjoyment is for hereafter. It is, then, a gift that can be received forthwith by those of good will (10: 14), and yet a realm that must be 'entered', equivalent to the heavenly world and salvation (10: 23–26). All therefore comes from God as a free gift, to be freely accepted, and leads to God and to that glory of which the Transfiguration gives the consoling presage—of that new world where Jesus will 'drink a new wine with his disciples' (14: 25).

Our Lord is called Son of God, the Christ, Son of David, and names Himself by preference 'Son of Man'. In his very first line, St Mark calling Him 'Christ', and 'Son of God', shows that they do not mean for him the same thing. Evil spirits recognize Him as both holy and super-human (1: 25; 3: 11; 5: 7. In 1: 34 'Christ' should not be read: it is in a few MSS only). But our Lord refuses their testimony: *they* should not be His witnesses! But the supreme sanction is given by the Father Himself to His Son—at the Baptism (1: 11) and at the Transfiguration (9: 7): in the parable of the keepers of the vineyard, He designates Himself as the only, beloved Son (12: 6): and in the vision of the Second Coming He is above all the angels—'*His*' angels—in regard of the Father (13: 32): and before Caiphas He acknowledges His Divinity though to do so meant His doom (14: 62). Though 'Son of God' *in itself* need not mean quite simply 'God', in St Mark's title to his gospel and in its context later on, it certainly means that Jesus is true Son of God, as we believe Him to be, and as St Paul so emphatically declared Him to be.

It is remarkable that the disciples, wondering who Jesus might be, thought of Elias, a new prophet, and so forth, but *not* the 'Messias' (6: 15): when Simon exclaimed 'Thou art the Christ' (7: 29), St Matthew explains that he had had this revealed to him by God, and contrasts him with the others (Matt. 16: 17). In fact, our Lord urgently insisted that they were not to make Him known as 'the Christ'—doubtless that title would have awoken nationalist enthusiasm; and if He did not rebuke Bartimaeus who hailed Him as Son of David (10: 47) nor the crowds on Palm Sunday when they cried that in Him the throne (i.e. dynasty) of David was reappearing (11: 10), well, the end was approaching: He did not shrink from showing that the Messias was not *only* David's 'son' but his Lord (12: 35): only at the very last He claimed Messiah-ship (14: 62), and it was because manifestly, they thought, He had rejected that claim, that they mocked Him on the Cross (15: 32).

Now if, as some have held, 'Son of Man' was popularly accepted as equivalent with 'Messias', our Lord who from the outset called Himself so would have been proclaiming Himself Messias, which is the opposite of the truth. 'Son of

Man' can mean simply 'man': (Ps. 8: 5) 'What is man that thou art mindful of him? The son of man, that thou visitest him?' An angel repeatedly addresses Ezechiel as 'O son of man?', as though, maybe, he emphasizes the prophet's mere human estate, in view of the lofty mission assigned to him. There was also the great vision related in Daniel 7, where, after the apparition of four 'beasts', representing successive pagan 'empires', there appears a form 'like unto a son of man', i.e. in human, not bestial, shape. To *him* is given a universal kingdom and everlasting power never to be destroyed. But Daniel definitely says that the possessor of this kingdom is a 'collectivity'—the People of the Saints, nor did this prophecy ever cause the expression 'Son of Man' to become current as meaning 'the Messias'.[1] Certainly our Lord means by it *Himself*, 'I'. And He uses it in two ways: to mean that *He* has power to forgive sins, to dispense from rules about the Sabbath (2: 10, 28), and that He will come in glory as judge of mankind (8: 38; 13: 26); but also, that He is truly human, destined to suffer and to die (8: 31; 9: 12, 30; 10: 33ᵃ 45; 14: 21, 41). He has essentially come to *serve* (10: 45). Neither St Mark, nor St Matthew nor St Luke, naturally, uses terms of Greek philosophy such as Nature, Person, Substance or *define* the Son of God made Man as later theologians would. But St Mark shows Him as experiencing all that a true man does—He is hungry, tired and sleeps; He is indignant, surprised, compassionate, loving; He endures the distress and grief and bewilderment proper to his Agony; on the cross He triumphs over His sense of utter dereliction (e.g., 1: 41; 6: 34; 9: 22; 10: 16, 21; 14: 34); He needs to 'humanize' His knowledge by enquiry, gaining 'experimental' knowledge (5: 30; 8: 5; 9: 16, 21, 33), though He reads hearts and knows the future (13: 1, 9; 14: 9, etc.). Above all, He places Himself at the centre of human life. He does not say only: 'Serve God!'

---

[1] Doubtless, to the Jewish mind a Kingdom implied a King. But we do not think Daniel had a person in mind here, or that 'a son of man' here represented a historical person.

but, 'Follow *me*'—and we must do so whomsoever else we shall leave behind, even though His Way of the Cross leads Him, and therefore us, to death. But death is not the end: He rises again, and the final goal is Life Everlasting. Here we rejoin the central teaching of St John and of St Paul.

It has been said that we should compare Mark with St Peter's first sermon to the Gentiles (Acts 10: 37–42); but St Peter will hardly have remembered or St Luke have recorded verbatim a speech made so long ago. The *substance* only can have been recalled, and cast into Luke's own style. St Peter says that our Lord was anointed by the Holy Ghost and with *power* (which no doubt includes 'miracles' but must also refer to His way of preaching 'with authority'), and St Luke's words 'he went about doing good' are compared with Mark 7: 37, where the people say 'he hath done all things well'. It is true that St Mark alludes in his short document to 15 out of the 20 miracles recorded by St Matthew and adds 2, and that these are more vividly related than Matthew's are. Notice that these cover the whole field—e.g. inanimate nature (stilling the sea; multiplying the bread); when asked for, or without request; when faith was exacted, or merely praised; when done by mere command, or by touch, or by some symbolical act, or gradually.[1] Be clear that we are not bound to think that all our Lord's cures were *wholly* supernatural: some may have been due to His supernatural power combined with natural suggestion (as when He took hold of the sufferer's hand, or used a 'ceremonial' act like touching eyes or tongue with saliva, or acted at a distance (the Syrophoenician's daughter), but not, when He e.g. raised the dead. In somewhat the same way, we may suppose that when sufferers are said to be possessed by, or have, or 'be in' an evil spirit, a *mixture* of physical sickness and influence (greater or less) of an evil spirit may be surmised. It is not true that the Jews thought all illnesses the result of 'posses-

[1] See Analysis of the Miracles, at end of Introduction, p. xxvi.

sion', as we say: no one suggested that Lazarus, our Lord's friend, was possessed, though he was sick and died of his illness! Again, a bodily infirmity, or weakness of mind, may as it were give a handle to an evil spirit wishful to control the sufferer. It is evident that the boy cured after the Transfiguration (9: 16–28) gave every symptom of epilepsy: but our Lord no less evidently *assumes* 'possession', commands the evil spirit to come out of him, and adds: 'This kind goeth not out save by prayer and fasting', practices which have nothing to do with a mere cure of epilepsy; nor could 'faith', which was demanded—not from the boy but from his father—have been mere 'self-suggestion', because neither would that have influenced the boy. In short, when the Scriptures make it clear that our Lord worked a *miracle*, and addressed an evil spirit as such, we have grounds for being sure that a miracle was worked, and an evil spirit driven away.[1]

IV GENERAL OUTLINE OF THE GOSPEL ACCORDING TO SAINT MARK

We have, then, as background, a simple Roman lodging, where St Peter, no longer young, lived with St Mark, his companion and assistant. St Peter had never become acclimatized to Latin or even Greek culture: he thought in Aramaic and his heart was still in Palestine where his impetuous youth had been spent, and where he had lived those years which had transformed him. Now, as he knew death was nearing (2 Peter 1: 14), this incident or that may have faded from his memory, but, as often happens for older men, other things will have stood out more than ever vividly in his mind, so that in his teaching, and in what the clumsy-fingered St Mark faithfully wrote down, we seem to be aware of one who *sees* what he says.

St Peter proposed to teach the Gospel, the Good Message,

[1] Teachers may refer to the passage by Mgr Catherinet on the demoniacs of the gospels in *Satan* (English tr., Sheed and Ward).

of Jesus Christ, the Son of God, and Mark duly starts from the 'beginning' of this—the apparition of the Baptist, and the Baptism of our Lord. Thus Old and New Testament are welded together; and the Voice from Heaven and the Descent of the Holy Spirit set their seal upon Him who came into our world, True Man, as He was True God. Even so, He endured first to be 'tested' by the devil in the wilderness, but refused to accept a life of any self-seeking, of worldly glory and power, nor indeed was He ever to work a miracle merely on His own behalf. Further, He waited till the Baptist had been imprisoned and the heralding Voice was silenced. Then our Lord began His public Ministry, preaching in synagogues as any Jew might do, but with 'authority', as no other dared to do. And He corroborates His forceful words by 'works of power'—He expels an evil spirit from a haunted man (for after all His work is to be in essence spiritual); but men are 'body' too! He gently lifts back to health the fevered woman in Simon's house and she serves food to them: He does not hesitate to touch the poor leper who appeals to Him: they break through a roof rather than that the paralytic on his mattress should not reach Him: He calls to Him the despised tax-collector and goes to his house for the feast that the grateful man has arranged for Him. But almost at once the Scribes and Pharisees distil their drop of poison into the fresh sweetness of these first days: He *should* not have mixed with St Matthew's 'sinful' associates: He should not have touched the leper, He should not have cured the withered hand or picked ears of corn upon the Sabbath—He *looked round at them* with grief and indignation: yes! the Son of Man could forgive sins even upon earth, was Lord also of the Sabbath, was that Bridegroom during whose presence His friends might not fast. In short, He made it clear that the robes of the Old Testament had become threadbare; the skins that contained that old wine had worn through: the moral law of God was imperishable, but those who should have been its guardians and heralds had stifled it beneath innumerable observances, till the ordinary Jew might well despair of 'walking in the way of righteousness'.

Our Lord continues His life of powerful yet loving miracles, each with special vividly-touched-on detail—like those proper to the story of the raising of Jairus's little daughter; the cure of the poor woman too shy to do more, till she was called, than catch hold of a fringe of our Lord's cloak; of that other pagan woman who agreed that she had right to no more than the crumbs fallen from the children's table; those more dramatically related acts, like the expulsion of the evil spirits from the Gadarene demoniac or the cure of the epileptic boy; and those which show His lordship over nature—when He walks on the waters, stills the storm and multiplies the bread.

But all the while, by word as well as act, He was uttering His Message. He began by trying to change hearts, from the mere exterior observance of ritual to a more spiritual worship. Then, He turns to the ancient hope for a Kingdom of God— a Triumph of the Lord among His People; and this too He spiritualizes, by means of those parables which He spoke so gently, tempering His message to the intelligence of those who were listening.

Yet in some ways He had been making them wonder *who He was*. He spoke with authority, but they wondered whence came that authority? He would not provide them with an excuse for thinking He claimed to be the longed-for Messias: yet He certainly used the ambiguous title 'Son of Man' as somehow meaning peculiarly Himself, and had said that He had power on earth to forgive sins. However, when John the Baptist was martyred, and men began to say that Jesus was John brought back to life, it became evident that He must try to drive home to His closest associates alike who He was and what must be His destiny. For He had first attracted to His company, then definitely *called*, those Twelve who should carry on His work, in His Name and with His delegated power. It was St Peter who declared that

He was the Christ—yet, it was he who forthwith began with horror to repudiate our Lord's affirmation that He must be rejected and die. And this acknowledgement of St Peter's, followed by the Transfiguration and the divine Voice that then was heard, meant the opening of the last part of our Lord's ministry as truly as the Baptism opened its beginning.

From now on, our Lord devoted Himself more earnestly than ever to the training of the Apostles, though never could He make the approach of His passion and death win their conviction. A strange mingling of austerity and tenderness is seen in all this last 'chapter' but one: His love for little children; His recognition of the widow's tiny gift in the Temple: His acceptance of the pouring of ointment upon His head—a loving act, unconsciously anticipating that burial now so near. We need no more emphasize how much our Lord Himself dwells upon the series—rejection, death, resurrection, and glorious advent, nor how the following of Him includes the taking up of a cross, the renouncing of self, and service along with Him. Nor need we dwell on that mysterious discourse in which the imminent siege and sack of Jerusalem is but a symbol of the judgement upon this world and its passing away.

No guidance is needed from the Supper Room in which the New Alliance was once and for all ratified in our Lord's own Body and Blood, to Gethsemani, and the successive 'Stations' of the Passion till Calvary is reached, and indeed St Mark's simple narrative is best read by those who are on their knees. What amplification may be desired, will be found in the other Evangelists and their special contributions.

ANALYSIS OF THE MIRACLES

The letters M, L, mean that the miracle is recorded also in Matthew and Luke. The letters *a* means that faith was praised; *b*, that it was exacted; *c*, that the miracle was asked for; *d*, that it was unasked; *e*, that it was worked by a simple command; *f*, that it was wrought by touch; *g*, that a symbolical gesture was added; *h*, that it was wrought gradually.

Over diseases:

1. Simon's wife's mother (1: 29–31; M., L., c., f.).
2. The leper in Galilee (1: 40–45; M., L., c., f.).
3. The sick of the palsy (2: 3–12; M., L., a., c., e.).
4. The withered hand (3: 1–5; M., L., d., e.).
5. The issue of blood (5: 23–24; M., L., a., f.).
6. The deaf and dumb man (7: 32–37; c., g.).
7. The blind man at Bethsaida (8: 22–26; c., h.).
8. Bartimaeus (10: 46, 52; M., L., a., c., e.).

Over evil spirits:

9. The demoniac at Capharnaum (1: 23–26; L., d., e.).
10. The Gadarene demoniac (5: 2–15; M., L., d., e.).
11. The Syrophoenician's daughter (7: 25–30; M., a., c., e.)
12. The demoniac boy (9: 16–28; M., L., b., c., d.).

Over life and death:

13. Jairus's daughter (5: 22, 23, 35–43; M., L., b., c., f.).

Over Nature:

14. Stilling the storm (4: 37–40; M., L., c., e.).
15. Feeding the 5,000 (6: 31–44; M., L., d., f.).
16. Walking on the waters (6: 47–51; M., d.).
17. Feeding the 4,000 (8: 2–9; M., d., f.).

THE PARABLES

1. The new cloth; the new wine (2: 22–23; M., L.).
2. The sower (4: 1–20; M., L.).
3. The candle and the bushel (4: 21, 22; M., L.).
4. The seed growing secretly (4: 26–29).
5. The mustard seed (4: 30–32; M., L.).
6. The wicked husbandmen (12: 1–8; M., L.).
7. The fig-tree (13: 28, 29; M., L.).

VERSIONS REFERRED TO

The Septuagint (LXX); the Greek version of the Old Testament (O.T.).

The Vulgate (Vg.); the Latin version of both O. and N. Testaments.

The Douay Version, made from the Vg. at Rheims and Douay, 1582–1610. This is the text used in this series.

The Authorized and Revised Versions (A.V. and R.V.) are those used in the Church of England and other denominations.

NOTE ON SCRIBES, PHARISEES, SADDUCEES

These names occur so often in the Gospels that it may be simplest to say once and for all what they stand for.

The Scribes.   For the Jew, religion meant the 'Law', and the Law meant the rules for life written down, it was held, by Moses. The Scribes, though not priests, were more and more important as interpreters of the Law: true, they might not always agree—there were 'schools of thought' among them, some more rigid, some more lax. In point of fact, it was they who accumulated a mass of regulations which they claimed to be the proper way of applying the Law to actual circumstances. Such were the rules concerning the Sabbath, fasting, the washing of hands; clean or unclean foods, objects or persons. Thus an intolerable yoke was laid on the consciences of would-be law-abiding Jews.

The Pharisees, which means 'Separatists'—a name that may have been given to them at first as a mere nickname, like 'Christian' itself—numbered, it is thought, about 6,000, and plumed themselves on not being 'as other men are', even their fellow-Jews. They professed to obey all the rules laid down by the Scribes, and many of them made a public display of their observances. Hence, if they really did act up to their profession, they were apt to become intolerably proud; if they did not, they were hypocrites, and it is by no means only our Lord who called them so. They were inclined to be nationalists, and in fact (Josephus tells us: he lived from 37 to about A.D. 100) they refused to take an oath of allegiance to the Emperor Augustus or to King Herod the Great.

Their tragedy was, that while officially representing the ancestral religion, and insisting on the purity of its observances, they turned it into something quite beyond what the ordinary Jew, even pious, could practise.

The Sadducees claimed to derive their name from Zadok, the high-priest in the days of Solomon. It is certain that they adhered more or less closely to the heirs of the Maccabees who had developed a priest-king line. They were, on the whole, 'aristocrats', the Pharisees belonged more to the 'middle-class'. But they took second place in popular esteem, so impressive had the Pharisees made themselves: besides, it was known that the Sadducees were 'broad-minded', if not lax; they disbelieved in a spiritual world of angels, and in personal survival. They would have wished to be on good terms with the pagan governments of the day. It is clear how, in different ways, these three groups were bound to find themselves opposed to our Lord.[1]

[1] Many amusing and enlightening anecdotes about these people can be found in Dr J. P. Arendzen's *Prophets, Priests and Publicans*, though this book appeared so long ago as 1926.

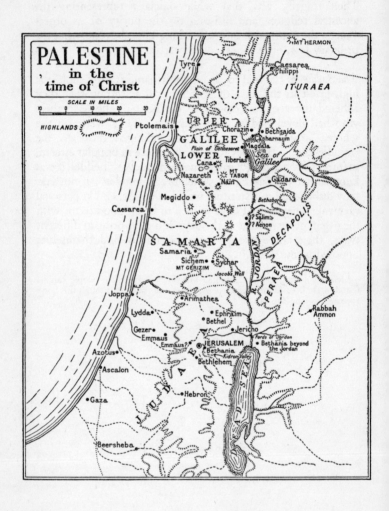

PALESTINE
in the
time of Christ

SCALE IN MILES
10   0   10   20   30

HIGHLANDS

MT HERMON

Tyre

Caesarea
Philippi

ITURAEA

Ptolemais

UPPER
GALILEE

Chorazin   Bethsaida
          Capharnaum
Plain of Gennesaret   Magdala

LOWER

Cana   Tiberias   Sea of
                        Galilee
Nazareth   MT
              TABOR
              Naim   Gadara

Megiddo

Bethabara

Caesarea   ?Salim
                                  ?Aenon

SAMARIA   DECAPOLIS

Samaria

Sicheme   Sychar
MT GERIZIM
              Jacob's Well

Joppa

          Arimathea

Lydda   Ephraim
                   Bethel

Gezer   Jericho
    Emmaus   Fords of Jordan
       Emmaus? JERUSALEM   Bethania beyond
Azotus   Bethania   the Jordan
                Kidron Valley
          Bethlehem

Ascalon   Rabbah
                                      Ammon

          Hebron

Gaza

JUDAEA

PERAEA

R. JORDAN

DEAD SEA

Beersheba

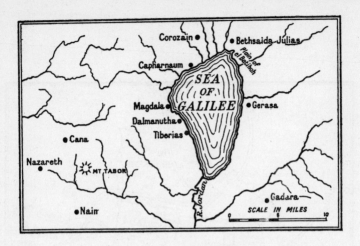

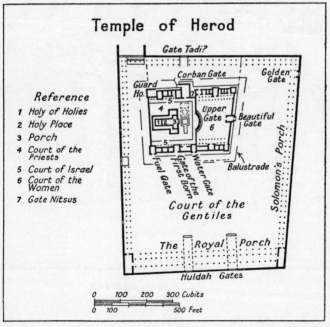

Temple of Herod

Gate Tadi?

Corban Gate

Golden Gate

Guard Ho.

Upper Gate

Beautiful Gate

Water Gate

Gate of the First Born

Fuel Gate

Balustrade

Solomon's Porch

Court of the Gentiles

The Royal Porch

Huldah Gates

Reference
1 Holy of Holies
2 Holy Place
3 Porch
4 Court of the Priests
5 Court of Israel
6 Court of the Women
7 Gate Nitsus

0   100   200   300 Cubits

0   100   500 Feet

By permission of S.P.C.K.

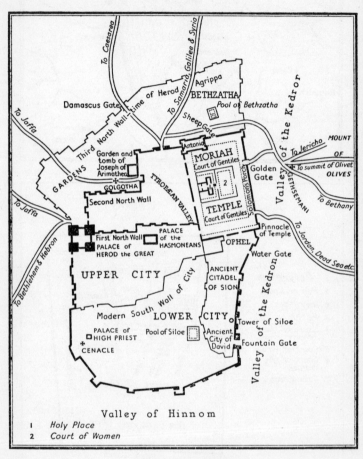

PLAN OF JERUSALEM

xxxii

SAINT MARK

CHAPTER ONE

The Beginning of the Gospel: 1–4
(cf. Matt. 3: 1–4; Luke 3: 1–6)

1. The beginning of the gospel of Jesus Christ, the Son of God.
2. As it is written in Isaias the prophet: *Behold I send my angel before thy face who shall prepare the way before thee.*

1, 2. St Mark wishes to say that the beginning of the Good News █████ut Jesus Christ was the preaching of the Baptist: cf. Acts 1: █, 10: 37. (The word εὐαγγέλιον occurs 8 times in Mark, 4 in Matthew, not in Luke, twice only in Acts though not in Luke's own narrative; often in St Paul and always in the sense of 'good news', i.e. the new good doctrine of salvation.) He corroborates his assertion by recalling that Isaias had foretold this preaching (Isaias 40: 3). But the words of this prophet begin only in verse 3—'a voice of one crying, etc.' The previous words are from Malachias, 3: 1. The difficulty was noticed in the earliest times and St Mark was actually reproached for not knowing his Old Testament. The simplest explanation is this—Matt. (9: 10) and Luke (7: 27) both quote the words of Malachias (without naming him), in connection with the Baptist and make three changes from the LXX text of which the most important is that they write 'thy face' and 'before thee' instead of the original 'my' and 'me'. Mark's sentence contains exactly the same changes. Probably, then, some early writer, remembering the words about the Baptist in Matthew and Luke, added

3. *A voice of one crying in the desert: Prepare ye the way of the Lord, make straight his paths.*

4. John was in the desert, baptizing and preaching the baptism of penance, unto remission of sins.

The Preaching of the Baptist: 5–8
(Matt. 3: 5–6, 11, 12; Luke 3: 15–16)

5. And there went out to him all the country of Judea and all they of Jerusalem and were baptized by him in the river of Jordan, confessing their sins.

---

them to Mark's text, perhaps in the margin and not intending that they should interrupt (as they do) the statement 'as it is written in Isaias' and the quotation of what is written.

3. Probably this verse should be punctuated: 'The voice of one crying: 'Prepare, in the desert, the road of the Lord! Make smooth his paths!' Before the arrival of important ▮▮ abo; roads (even recently) were repaired: but always the ▮▮ 27: regarded the 'preparation' for the 'Coming' of the Lord as something 'moral', not just material—a change of hearts, not a mere smoothing of roads. It is in this sense that we must interpret John's exhortation to 'repentance'.

4. The 'desert', no doubt the region S.E. of Jerusalem, in which John preached was constantly crossed by caravans; and it was easy for him to come down, for 'baptisms', to the Jordan— that extraordinary stream that rises 1,300 feet above sea-level, often amid the snows, only to end 1,300 feet below, and to expire amid the steams of the Dead Sea. John's 'baptism' did not remit sins, but prepared men to feel the contrition which would issue into their forgiveness. A ritual bath, not only among Jews but among many pagans, symbolized the getting clean from a bad past and the adoption of a purer life hereafter. The difference between even John's baptism and Christ's—the former indicating only a 'moral' change and the latter something super-natural—will soon be seen.

6. And John was clothed with camel's hair, and a leathern girdle about his loins: and he ate locusts and wild honey.

7. And he preached, saying: There cometh after me one mightier than I, the latchet of whose shoes I am not worthy to stoop down and loose.

8. I have baptized you with water: but he shall baptize you with the Holy Ghost.

---

5. St Luke (3) shows that this 'confession of sins' was no mere acknowledgement that John's penitents were 'sinful' since he gave detailed 'spiritual advice' to different sorts of men.

6. John's dress of 'camel's hair' was that of the ancient prophets (4 Kings 1: 8; Zach. 13: 4): i.e. his cloak was woven of this: camel's *hide* would have been too stiff to make a dress of. The 'girdle of skin' was underneath this. The locusts that he ate were not 'locust beans', as some have suggested: Arabs still eat locusts after pulling off head, wings and tail, though they make them into a sort of paste with butter and salt, which John could not have obtained. The 'wild honey' was probably a sort of gum exuded by such shrubs (e.g. tamarisks) as could grow in the desert. Possibly, however, it was the sort of honey that wild bees stored in the crannied rocks.

7. John makes it clear that his is not the 'absolute' baptism: 'The Stronger than he' was to follow him, and John declared that he was not worthy to 'stoop down' and unloose the strap of the sandals of the Messias. (St Matthew merely says: 'to carry' his sandals.) The act was so humble that even a Jewish slave could not legally be forced to perform it. John's baptism was only an external pouring of water, symbolizing no doubt purification and stimulating recipients to contrition: but the future would contain an inpouring of the Holy Spirit, which in the O.T. always meant the giving of courage, wisdom and all sorts of heavenly graces, especially in Messianic times: e.g. Isaias 44: 3; Joel 3: 1; Zach. 12: 10; 13: 1: Matthew and Luke add 'and with fire'; this was proverbial for a purification more drastic than that of water (cf. Num. 31: 23): Mark omits what forecasts the Judgement.

3

The Baptism of our Lord: 9–11

(Matt. 3: 13–17; Luke 3: 21–22; John 1: 31–34)

9. And it came to pass, in those days, Jesus came from Nazareth of Galilee and was baptized by John in the Jordan.

10. And forthwith coming up out of the water, he saw the heavens opened and the Spirit as a dove, descending and remaining on him.

---

9. 'In those days' means no more than 'then', i.e. while John was baptizing. Nazareth was a small town on the south-west slopes of the mountains of Galilee. St John (1: 28) says that our Lord came to Bethania beyond (i.e. across) the Jordan; but since this place cannot be identified, it remains probable that He came south from His home-town to wherever John usually baptized, which was, very likely, one end or the other of a ford near Jericho.

10. 'Immediately' ($\epsilon\dot{\upsilon}\theta\dot{\upsilon}s$) is as favourite a word of St Mark's as 'then' ($\tau\acute{o}\tau\epsilon$) is of St Matthew. As a rule each remains vague, though here it does seem to mean 'forthwith', while our Lord was actually coming up out of the river. The skies were 'torn apart' ($\sigma\chi\acute{\iota}\zeta\epsilon\sigma\theta\alpha\iota$ is a strong word). 'He saw' must here refer to Jesus: in John it is the Baptist who sees: St Matthew ('*This* is my beloved Son' instead of 'Thou art') suggests that the heavenly voice was addressed to all. Presumably men saw, and heard, what their souls were 'attuned to' (cf. John 12: 29, 30, where after a Voice from heaven had spoken, some said 'it thundered', others, 'an angel spoke to him': our Lord said: 'This Voice came not because of me, but for your sakes'). As for the vision of the Holy Spirit 'as a dove', a supernatural vision even when taking an 'imagina-tive' form need not be seen by all—thus at Lourdes or Fatima, St Bernadette and the children 'saw' our Lady but nobody else did. But why should the Spirit manifest Himself as a 'dove'? The dove was used symbolically in the O.T. in many ways; but we think it is certain that here what is remembered is the Spirit of God descending on to and brood-

4

11. And there came a voice from heaven: Thou art my beloved Son; in thee I am well pleased.

The Temptation in the Wilderness: 12–13
(Matt. 4: 1–11; Luke 4: 1–13)

12. And immediately the Spirit drove him out into the desert.
13. And he was in the desert forty days and forty nights, and was tempted by Satan. And he was with beasts: and the angels ministered to him.

---

ing over the formless, lifeless waste of waters (Gen. 1: 2) and giving the first impulse to the history of the world. The immense solemnity of this event is due to its being the official beginning of our Lord's Ministry. By baptizing Him, John completed his own ministry: the Old Testament came to an end.

11. The Father and the Holy Spirit testified to what our Lord *was*, and in their Name and power He went forth to His saving work. The Flood too may possibly be recalled.

12, 13. 'Immediately' ($\epsilon\dot{v}\theta\dot{v}s$) occurs ten times in this one chapter. The Greek is more vivid—'drives Him out' (see p. xxii): our Lord's human life was governed wholly by the Spirit. Mark does not mention that He fasted: but says simply: 'He was in the desert 40 days, being tempted by Satan.' The Vg. adds 'and 40 nights' to harmonize Mark with Matthew (4: 2) who wishes to make clear that our Lord's fast was uninterrupted. 'The Satan' means 'the Adversary'. St Mark enters into no details, but Matthew and Luke make it clear that the 'testing' of our Lord aimed at seeing whether He would use material means to accomplish His purpose. The 'beasts' can have been jackals, wolves, even panthers, and no doubt poisonous insects: St Mark does not mention them for dramatic effect, but to show that our Lord lived apart from all human contact: such 'ministry' as He received came from the service of angels.

The Beginning of Christ's Ministry: 14–15
(Matt. 4: 12–17; Luke 4: 14–15)

14. And after that John was delivered up, Jesus came into Galilee, preaching the gospel of the kingdom of God,

15. And saying: The time is accomplished and the kingdom of God is at hand. Repent and believe the gospel.

The Call of the First Four Disciples: 16–20
(Matt. 4: 18–22)

16. And passing by the sea of Galilee, he saw Simon and Andrew his brother, casting nets into the sea (for they were fishermen).

17. And Jesus said to them: Come after me; and I will make you to become fishers of men.

---

14. St Mark passes straight to what happens after the arrest of the Baptist (see 6: 17): Jesus comes to Galilee preaching (not 'to preach') 'the Gospel of God' (the Vg. adds 'the Kingdom')

15. which does not mean, here, the Good News *concerning* God, but the good news authorized by God, namely, that there is now no more delay: the future foretold by John is now the present; the Kingdom is drawn near, i.e. has arrived: enter into it by repentance and by faith. It is no more an affair of hope: it means entering into what is already here.

16. St Mark very often explains what he has just said, after he has said it, as here. He omits everything between the Temptation and this Galilean ministry and does not say that our Lord had already met Simon and Andrew in the south, and probably James and John (John 1: 35–51); but that encounter had not been a definite 'vocation'. The word ἀμφιβάλλοντες shows that they were using a special kind of cast-net called ἀμφίβληστρον: it was large and circular and had a leaden weight attached to it; the fisherman would roll the net round his arm while keeping hold of the weight; then, with a sharp movement, he would make the net unroll and fall into the sea. Cf. Isaias 19: 8; Hab. 1: 17.

17. A very early hymn speaks to our Lord

18. And immediately leaving their nets, they followed him.
19. And going on from thence a little farther, he saw James the son of Zebedee and John his brother, who also were mending their nets in the ship:
20. And forthwith he called them. And leaving their father Zebedee in the ship with his hired men, they followed him.

Our Lord preaches in Capharnaum: 21-22

(Matt. 4: 13-16; Luke 4: 31)

21. And they entered into Capharnaum: and forthwith upon the sabbath days going into the synagogue, he taught them.

> Fisherman of mortals
> Who are being saved
> From the sea of evil,
> With sweetest life enticing
> Thy holy fish
> From the hostile wave.

19, 20. St Mark records St Peter's memories in the most natural way. St Peter remembers primarily that he and Andrew were fishing and does not think of saying they were in a boat: but, going a short way along the lake, he notices that James and John, 'they too', were in a boat, and then recalls that they were mending their nets, not fishing. He says, first, what meets the eye first, and then adds that these two brothers left not only their nets but their father, together with the 'hired men'—this does not mean that Zebedee was rich but rather the reverse: he had no regular staff of servants but hired men as need arose. Our Lord, then, is seen as from the outset associating others to Himself. His was not to be a solitary mission. Yet His new companions would need training—'I will make you *become* fishers of men'. This is the James who, we read in Acts 12: 2, was beheaded.

21. Capharnaum was a town on the west coast of the lake, towards the northern end. Its site has been identified with Tell

22. And they were astonished at his doctrine. For he was teaching them as one having power, and not as the scribes.

Hum where there are ruins of a synagogue, but these are said to be later than our Lord's time. Or else it may have been two miles farther south, at Khan-Minyeh, a centre of traffic, especially in fish, and likely to have a custom-house (Matt. 9: 1 ff.). When Nazareth rejected our Lord (Luke 4: 29), He came to feel that Capharnaum was 'his own city' (Matt. 4: 13; 9: 1). The plural, Sabbath-days (τοῖς σάββασιν), need not mean more than one Sabbath-day. τὰ σάββατα was the normal expression for 'the Sabbath day', i.e. the day of rest: not only Hebrew but the older Greek and Roman festivals were expressed by a neuter plural: *Anthesteria*; *Lupercalia*, etc. Legal sacrifices could be offered only in Jerusalem; but the need for *collective worship* is inherent in mankind. Jews would meet in the open air, e.g. by a river (Acts 16: 13), or, when possible, would build a 'synagogue', i.e. an 'assembly-place'. This was used not only for sabbath-worship, but as a school and for certain administrative purposes. At the back of the room on a dais was an 'Ark', veiled, and containing the scrolls of the Law and the Prophets. A lamp burned before this. In front of it were the seats, facing the people, of the 'elders' or rulers of the assembly, under a president. In the middle was a raised chair, and, after various prayers, the scrolls would be brought out and readings from the Law and the Prophets would follow and the singing of Psalms. Then any male Jew who could read Hebrew had the right to claim to recite and expound some passage from the Scripture. We see how the order of Mass, up to the sermon inclusively, is bequeathed to us from the synagogue system.

22. 'They were struck out of themselves' (with amazement): (ἐξεπλήσσοντο; cf. ἐκ-θαμβεῖσθαι, ἐκ-θαυμαζειν) this very strong word occurs 5 times in Mark: what so astounded His hearers was the absolute assurance with which our Lord spoke: He did not merely quote Scripture or tradition and the

8

Miracles in and around Capharnaum: 23–28

(Luke 4: 33–37)

23. And there was in their synagogue a man with an unclean spirit; and he cried out,

24. Saying: What have we to do with thee, Jesus of Nazareth? Art thou come to destroy us? I know who thou art, the Holy One of God.

---

opinions of learned Rabbis, which was all the Scribes could do. We notice already His serene certainty about Himself: 'Follow *me*.' 'I will make you become fishers of men.' He could teach what was true, and could sway men's wills—though it does remain possible for our free will to resist divine grace.

23. The preaching is 'forthwith' sanctioned by a miracle. The man is described as being 'in' ($\dot{\epsilon}\nu$) an unclean spirit (on 'possession', see p. xxii) when we might have expected '*in whom* was an unclean spirit'. But while the turn of phrase is merely a 'Hebraism' (cf. the woman 'in' an issue of blood: Mark 5: 25 and Luke 8: 43), here and elsewhere (e.g. 5: 2) it is hinted that the man's soul and the evil spirit as it were penetrated one another (see Rom. 8: 9. 'You are in the Spirit if the Spirit dwells in you'), and sometimes it is the possessing spirit who speaks, and sometimes the man who is possessed.

24. 'What to me and to thee' ($\tau i \ \dot{\eta} \mu \hat{\iota} \nu \ \kappa \alpha i \ \sigma o i$) does not mean: 'What hast thou in common with us?' but, 'Why are you interfering with us?' (cf. 2 Kings 16: 10; 19: 22; 4 Kings 9: 18. In John 2: 4, probably our Lord is telling his mother not to ask Him to anticipate the hour when His Messianic career, with its miracles, should begin). 'Art thou come to destroy us?' The spirit speaks in the plural—the whole power of evil spirits is endangered by Christ's advent into the world. Some prefer to read: 'Thou art come . . .': but the question is more dramatic than an assertion. 'The Holy One of God.' This does not necessarily imply that the evil spirit knew that our

9

25. And Jesus threatened him, saying: Speak no more, and go out of the man.

26. And the unclean spirit, tearing him and crying out with a loud voice, went out of him.

27. And they were all amazed, insomuch that they questioned among themselves, saying: What thing is this? What is this new doctrine? For with power he commandeth even the unclean spirits: and they obey him.

28. And the fame of him was spread forthwith into all the country of Galilee.

The Cure of Simon's Mother-in-Law: 29–31
(Matt. 8: 14–15; Luke 4: 38–39)

29. And immediately going out of the synagogue they came into the house of Simon and Andrew, with James and John.

Lord was divine, nor was the expression used of the Messias: it occurs only here, in Luke 4: 34 and John 6: 69. But it certainly shows how what is evil recognizes, and hates, what is pure and holy, and the evil spirit certainly recognizes a pre-eminence of holiness in Jesus.

25. ἐπετίμησεν means 'commanded' him, not 'threatened'; φιμώθητι strictly means 'be muzzled', but probably here is no more than an energetic order to keep silence.

26. 'Tearing him' (σπαράξαν) means that the evil spirit threw the man 'into convulsions', and then, with a cry of rage, set him free.

27. 'What is this? A new doctrine given with authority! and He commands the unclean spirits and they obey Him!' The doctrine was 'new', not because of its contents, but because of the authoritative way in which it was taught. And now— it is guaranteed by a miracle!

28. 'The whole of the environment of Galilee' could mean either the whole country round about (Capharnaum), i.e. Galilee; or, the more normal sense of ἡ περίχωρος, the country round about Galilee.

30. And Simon's wife's mother lay in a fit of a fever: and forthwith they tell him of her.

31. And coming to her, he lifted her up, taking her by the hand; and immediately the fever left her, and she ministered unto them.

Many Miracles: 32–34
(Matt. 8: 16–17; Luke 4: 40–41)

32. And when it was evening, after sunset, they brought to him all that were ill and that were possessed with devils.

33. And all the city was gathered together at the door.

34. And he healed many that were troubled with divers diseases. And he cast out many devils: and he suffered them not to speak, because they knew him.

---

31. Courtesy and affection cause the two brothers to invite our Lord to their house and meal: it would have been gravely impolite to exclude James and John. The sick woman was lying in the women's part of the house—St Mark does not profess to give an exhaustive account of the situation, nor need we ask, with St Jerome, where Peter's wife was (he concludes she was already dead! Let us hope she was there, comforting her mother even if she could not cure her). The scene is beautifully visualized: the offered hospitality; the immediate mention of the sick woman; our Lord's entry into her room, helping her to rise—cured; and—what more realistic?—her forthwith seeing to their meal!

32. Till sunset, the Sabbath was not over, and it would have been forbidden to carry the sick even to a doctor.

33. Oriental twilight is brief; everyone wanted a cure before night fell: hence the crowd round Simon's door.

34. 'All' had been brought; but He cured 'many'. This need not mean that He *could* not cure all (unless indeed their spiritual state prevented Him), or that He chose a certain number: but simply that a great crowd had come and He did in fact cure a great number. St Luke 4: 41, writes: 'they knew that He was the Christ'; the word is added here in a few MSS. for the sake

The Preaching Throughout Galilee: 35-39
(Luke 4: 42-43)

35. And rising very early, going out, he went into a desert place: and there he prayed.
36. And Simon and they that were with him followed after him.
37. And when they had found him, they said to him: All seek for thee.
38. And he saith to them: Let us go into the neighbouring towns and cities, that I may preach there also; for to this purpose am I come.
39. And he was preaching in their synagogues and in all Galilee and casting out devils.

---

of harmony with Luke. The evil spirits recognized our Lord as belonging to a supernatural spiritual world, but not necessarily that He was the Messias.

35. 'Very early, while it was still dark', Vg.: diluculo valde ($\pi\rho\omega\grave{\iota}$ ἔννυχα λίαν). 'Desert' means no more than 'solitary'. It is not true that our Lord prayed only for our example. Nor is prayer only petition, but gratitude and adoration. St Thomas says: 'But because there is in Christ, first, the divine will, and again, the human will, the human will is not efficacious to carry out what it wills, save through divine power; hence it is that it is right that Christ (competit Christo), in so far as He is man and has a human will, should pray.'

36. The disciples κατεδίωξεν, almost, 'hunted him down'.

38. κωμοπόλεις (a word occurring only here) does not mean towns and cities, but probably 'townlets', large villages. 'For unto this came I forth—ἐξῆλθον.' It would be rather flat to suppose this means: 'that is why I left your house': St Luke (4: 43) says: 'for it is unto that that I have been sent', which suggests that St Mark too alludes to his coming forth from heaven into this world: Verbum supernum prodiens—Nec patris linquens dexteram. In John, it would certainly have this meaning: 8: 42; 13: 3; 16: 27, 30.

The Cure of a Leper: 40–45

(Matt. 8: 1–4; Luke 15: 12–16)

40. And there came a leper to him, beseeching him and kneeling down, said to him: If thou wilt thou canst make me clean.

41. And Jesus, having compassion on him, stretched forth his hand and touching him saith to him: I will. Be thou made clean.

42. And when he had spoken, immediately the leprosy departed from him: and he was made clean.

43. And he strictly charged him and forthwith sent him away.

44. And he saith to him: See thou tell no one; but go, shew thyself to the high priest and offer for thy cleansing the things that Moses commanded, for a testimony to them.

---

40. 'Leprosy' is a word covering various sorts of skin-diseases, from the terrible kind which attacks the joints so that whole fingers or even hands or feet may drop off, to the more hideous sort which attacks the nervous system and shows itself in red patches which turn white or black. True leprosy is not infectious, but other (even curable) sorts, like *tinea decalvans* which makes the hair fall off, are. It is not clear how far the Jews distinguished between these sorts of diseases (the regulations in Lev. 13 do not): we found, in the Transvaal, that the Boer farmers regarded any form of 'leprosy' as infectious. Anyhow, the Jew ruled that the 'leper' had to live outside towns (so did the Persians) and to cry out 'Unclean! unclean!' if one approached him or even if the wind blew from his direction. If the word ἐξέβαλεν, 'he thrust him out' (verse 43 and cf. 45), means more than 'sent him away', the leper had already technically offended by entering a house; in any case, our Lord had done so by touching him. But He who could drive away leprosy, could hardly be tainted by it!

43, 44. Jesus speaks *forcibly* to the man: His pity caused Him to work the miracle; but He neither wished to exempt him from the legal duty of getting a certificate from the priest

45. But he being gone out, began to publish and to blaze abroad the word: so that he could not openly go into the city, but was without in desert places. And they flocked to him from all sides.

('high Priest' is not in the Greek) so as to show it to 'them'— i.e. people who might feel dubious about the cure, for the scars would remain—nor yet to incur publicity, which, none the less, owing to the leper's disregarding His injunction, He did not avoid.

45. The 'word': either what our Lord had said to him, or, though St Mark does not so use the expression elsewhere, 'word' has the Hebrew sense of 'event'.

If it be asked why St Mark says nothing about the ministry in Jerusalem, which according to St John preceded that in Galilee, we may suppose (1) that St Mark was recording only St Peter's memories, and that St Peter had not been present in Jerusalem (but then neither do Matthew nor Luke mention the Jerusalem ministry): or (2) that St John followed a tradition of his own: or (3) that he did not always follow a chronological order, but arranged his material according to the doctrine and symbolism that he wished it to convey. E.g. we think he placed the cleansing of the Temple in a kind of 'introduction' to his narrative, whereas it actually occurred where the Synoptists say it did, during Holy Week.

CHAPTER TWO

The Cure of the Palsied Man: 1–12
(Matt. 9: 1–8; Luke 5: 17–26)

1. And again he entered into Capharnaum after some days.
2. And it was heard that he was in the house. And many came together, so that there was no room: no, not even at the door. And he spoke to them the word.
3. And they came to him, bringing one sick of the palsy, who was carried by four.
4. And when they could not offer him unto him for the multitude, they uncovered the roof where he was: and opening it, they let down the bed wherein the man sick of the palsy lay.

---

1. 'After some days' (δι' ἡμερῶν). After a space of days— 'In the house'—we are free to assume it was Simon's; anyhow, our Lord having returned secretly, He did not go into the streets.
2. So many people came in that there was 'no more' any room— even the doorway was packed with people. Orientals feel free to enter a neighbour's house. 'The word', i.e. His 'gospel'.
3. 'They come . . .' i.e. the relatives of the sick man, distinct from the 'four' who were carrying him: the detail 'four' marks an eye-witness; had the man been on a stretcher, two would have sufficed: but he was picked up just as he was, on his mattress, which would need one at each corner.
4. In simpler lake-side houses, of a single storey, roofs are still made thus—beams are laid from wall to wall, and sometimes other cross-beams upon these. Then comes a close-set covering of reeds or branches, and upon this, a layer of earth or

15

5. And when Jesus had seen their faith, he saith to the sick of the palsy: Son, thy sins are forgiven thee.

6. And there were some of the scribes sitting there and thinking in their hearts:

7. Why doth this man speak thus? He blasphemeth. Who can forgive sins, but God only?

8. Which Jesus presently knowing in his spirit that they so thought within themselves, saith to them: Why think you these things in your hearts?

9. Which is easier, to say to the sick of the palsy: Thy sins are forgiven thee; or to say: Arise, take up thy bed, and walk?

---

clay. St Luke (5: 19) speaks of tiles, which suggests that he visualized a Roman or Greek house rather than a Palestinian one. The latter, too, often have outside staircases. We hazard the suggestion that this house may have been a two-storeyed one and that it was the roof of the top storey which was taken off, when the bed could have been taken down an interior staircase without difficulty; else how could the crowd have tolerated a shower of clay and twigs pouring down on their heads?

5. 'Their faith', i.e. that of the relatives or the carriers. Possibly there is a sort of ellipse—the sick man's faith led him at once to sorrow for his sins, especially as illness, etc., was generally regarded among the Jews as punishment for sin: cf. Job. Hence our Lord's kind word 'Son'—almost 'my child'—Matt. 9: 2: adds 'have confidence!' θάρσει. The present tense suggests that the sins are at that moment forgiven, but our Lord avoids saying point-blank: 'I forgive you your sins' though that is how the Scribes, *seated* there (in the place of honour?), took it. 'Who can forgive sins, save *one*—God!'

8. 'Knowing clearly (ἐπιγνούς) in His spirit': a direct reading of *hearts*, different from the outside observation noted in verse 5, cf. 8: 12.

9. The argument is really addressed to onlookers. It is easier to *say*: 'Your sins are forgiven' (because no one can see what

16

10. But that you may know that the Son of man hath power on earth to forgive sins (he saith to the sick of the palsy):

11. I say to thee: Arise. Take up thy bed and go into thy house.

12. And immediately he arose and, taking up his bed, went his way in the sight of all; so that all wondered and glorified God, saying: We never saw the like.

The Call of Levi, or Matthew: 13–17
(Matt. 9: 9–13; Luke 5: 27–32)

13. And he went forth again to the sea side: and all the multitude came to him. And he taught them.

---

happens), but harder to say: 'Arise, etc.', because a visible result is demanded, and if nothing happens, the previous declaration would evidently be valueless. But a startling exterior sign would lead the onlookers to accept what was not only 'harder' but on a different plane altogether—the fact that sins were forgiven, and by Jesus Himself. And indeed verse 12 shows that they were 'out of themselves' with astonishment because of the miracle they had *seen*. 'The people' makes no allusion to the forgiveness of sins, nor to the words.

10. 'That you may know that the Son of Man has full authority, on earth, to forgive sins . . .'. Possibly these words were spoken softly, so as to reach only the Scribes to whom indeed they were addressed. Our Lord did not yet intend to reveal Himself publicly as the Messias, nor did the apparition (Daniel 7: 13) of 'one like to a son of man' (i.e. in human form) mean explicitly the 'Messias'. See on this p. xx. It does not seem that the Scribes will have understood our Lord as saying anything more than: 'That you may realize that I, on earth, have authority to forgive sins, as God, in heaven, has', and that will have shocked them quite as much as if our Lord had said: 'I, the Son of Man', i.e. the Messias . . .', etc.

13. Again: cf. 1: 45 rather than 1: 16. Our Lord would seem to have given up any attempt at privacy: we cannot suppose that

14. And when he was passing by, he saw Levi, the son of Alphaeus, sitting at the receipt of custom; and he saith to him: Follow me. And rising up, he followed him.

15. And it came to pass that as he sat at meat in his house, many publicans and sinners sat down together with Jesus and his disciples. For they were many, who also followed him.

He preached only once or twice from the lake-side: the point of going there was that He could not be crushed on all sides by the crowd.

14. The 'customs' ($\tau\epsilon\lambda\acute{\omega}\nu\iota o\nu$) were exacted here on both exports and imports (*portorium*) and maybe also a tax permitting men to pass from the territory of Herod Antipas to that of his brother Philip, etc. These kinglets had general customs-officers who farmed out the actual collection of taxes to subordinates, whose duty it was to denounce those who tried to escape taxation, but who also had every chance of exaggerating the amounts properly due, since there was no system of making these known with certainty. Levi is the same as Matthew, as St Matthew himself names him: he was the author of the first gospel, and possibly brother of St James the 'Less': it was not rare for a Jew to have two names, one Jewish and one Latin or Greek, or indeed two Jewish. We should not over-dramatize this incident. We are not told that our Lord had never spoken to Levi before, nor that Levi left his moneys and accounts at the mercy of any chance passer-by or in confusion: doubtless he had a clerk.

15. Mark never makes unnecessary explanations—it is obvious that 'the' house was Levi's and that Levi invited Him to a dinner, and also with the only kind of associates he could find—even in classical Greek 'tax-collectors' are associated with men and women of loose morals: 'sinners' are almost habitually named along with tax-collectors (e.g. Matt. 9: 10, 11, 13; Luke 5: 30, 32, etc.). It was quite natural for Levi to invite our Lord to his house, as Simon did after his own vocation; His disciples came too, 'for' our Lord was followed

16. And the scribes and the Pharisees, seeing that he ate with publicans and sinners, said to his disciples: Why doth your master eat and drink with publicans and sinners?

17. Jesus hearing this, saith to them: They that are well have no need of a physician, but they that are sick. For I came not to call the just, but sinners.

The Disciples of the Baptist: 18–22
(Matt. 9: 14–17; Luke 5: 33–39)

18. And the disciples of John and the Pharisees used to fast. And they come and say to him: Why do the disciples of John and of the Pharisees fast; but thy disciples do not fast?

---

not only by the two or three who have been named, but by 'many'.

16. The Greek has οἱ γραμματεῖς τῶν Φαρισαίων which must mean 'the Scribes who belonged to the party of the Pharisees', unless words such as 'and some of' (the Pharisees)' have fallen out. 'Your master' is not in Mark, but simply: 'So then, he eats with tax-collectors, etc.?' Matthew adds 'your master', and seems to indicate that a number of disciples were not actually sharing in the meal, but collected, e.g., near the door. Our Lord, as He came out, could have heard what the critics were saying, and replied by using a current expression, not rare in Greek, to the effect that doctors go where they are needed, i.e. to the sick.

17. But 'I came, not to call the righteous, but sinners', cf. 1: 38, definitely alludes to our Lord's divine mission: it cannot mean merely that He came to Capharnaum, or even to Levi's house, in order to single out sinners for his help. In fact, all men are sinners and need salvation (Rom. 3: 23, etc.): He assumes, for the sake of argument, that the self-righteous Pharisees *are* righteous: well, then, they must not be surprised if He goes to others whom they judge to be sinful.

18. 'Were fasting' (St Luke generalizes: 'fast often'). Only the Day of Expiation was an obligatory fast-day for all (Lev. 16:

19. And Jesus saith to them: Can the children of the marriage fast as long as the bridegroom is with them? As long as they have the bridegroom with them, they cannot fast.

20. But the days will come when the bridegroom shall be taken away from them: and then they shall fast in those days.

21. No man seweth a piece of raw cloth to an old garment: otherwise the new piecing taketh away from the old, and there is made a greater rent.

29; cf. Acts 27: 9): devout Jews often fasted on Mondays and Thursdays (cf. the Pharisee in Luke 18: 12: 'I fast twice in the week'). But there were extra fasts on one of which our Lord's disciples were noticeably not fasting, while those of the Pharisees and the ascetic Baptist were. So 'people came' and asked Jesus why this was so.

19. Literally: 'the sons of the bridal chamber'. In Hebrew, 'sons, daughters, of . . .' merely indicates some connection with the next word. 'Daughters of the vine', i.e. its tendrils: 'sons of the thunderbolt'—John and James were regular thunderbolts! (3: 17). Here, all the friends of a bridegroom are meant: while he was there, fasting (a sign of grief, not festivity) was impossible. For our Lord as 'bridegroom of souls' see John 3: 29. Our Lord's bodily presence among His disciples is treated as a joyous marriage-feast.

20. Normally, it is the guests who leave the married pair. Here our Lord foresees His being 'taken away' from the visible companionship of His friends. Yet in the Christian life, though we are in one sense separated from our Lord, yet He is never *absent*, and joy must not be excluded from our contrition and penance.

21, 22. These two comparisons make our Lord's meaning wider and deeper. 'Raw' means unwashed, unshrunken cloth: no one stitches that on to an old dress: the moment it was washed the new cloth would shrink, and drag away more of the old cloth with it. So too, 'new', unfermented wine must not be put into old wine-skins worn thin, e.g. by rubbing against

22. And no man putteth new wine into old bottles: otherwise the wine will burst the bottles, and both the wine will be spilled and the bottles will be lost. But new wine must be put into new bottles.

The Sabbath Day: 23–28
(Matt. 12: 1–8; Luke 6: 1–5)

23. And it came to pass again, as the Lord walked through the corn fields on the sabbath, that his disciples began to go forward and to pluck the ears of corn.

24. And the Pharisees said to him: Behold, why do they on the sabbath day that which is not lawful?

---

the sides of mules. It would ferment and burst the skins and it and they would be lost. Our Lord was not merely explaining why His disciples did not observe the ritual fasts: but while He made it clear that He was not abolishing the everlasting moral law of God (Matt. 5: 17–20), He definitely teaches that something quite new—a new spirit and life—is to be given. This will break its way through the antiquated system within which Jewish religion had been imprisoned by the Scribes and Pharisees, so that even the Baptist's preaching and practice should be superseded.

23. 'Again' is in the Vg. only. Translate: 'And it happened that He was passing through the cornfields on the Sabbath day, and his disciples, as they went, began to pluck, etc.'

24. The rebuke was frivolous and malicious. A short walk was not forbidden on the Sabbath; it was always allowable to pick a few ears, or figs, or grapes beside a path; one might even pick wheat-ears on the Sabbath but not use a sickle (Deut. 23: 25). Our Lord could have mentioned this, but preferred to quote an Old Testament instance of a graver infringement of ceremonial rules. The Israelites (Lev. 24: 1–9) were to offer oil to burn all night before the Lord, and 12 loaves of bread which Aaron and his sons should 'set forth' before him, changing them every week and eating the old ones in the Sanctuary. A symbolical act of worship, owning that the

25. And he said to them: Have you never read what David did when he
had need and was hungry, himself and they that were with him?

26. How he went into the house of God, under Abiathar the high priest,
and did eat the loaves of proposition, which was not lawful to eat but
for the priests, and gave to them who were with him?

27. And he said to them: The sabbath was made for man, and not man for
the sabbath.

28. Therefore the Son of man is Lord of the sabbath also.

---

necessities of life come from God and must be referred back
to him. Now in 1 Kings 21: 1-6, we read that David came
to the priest Achimelech and begged for bread. The priest
said he had only 'holy bread', i.e. the sacred loaves that
were just being changed (verse 6), but though these strictly
belonged to the priests he would give them to David and his
hungry followers if they were ritually pure. But St Mark
says that the high-priest was Abiathar, who however became
so only later (2 Kings 21: 1). There are solutions of this
difficulty, e.g. that Achimelech had two names, but they all
lack evidence and seem artificial. St Mark is referring to the
story but not quoting it in detail; in fact the Old Testament
says that David came alone, and not that he entered the Holy
Place. St Mark is asserting one point only—that there is Old
Testament warrant for necessity over-riding ceremonial rules.
In English we cannot help saying 'Abiathar *the* high-priest'
but in the Greek versions the article is not always present. If it
is not, the words would certainly imply that Abiathar was
then high-priest; but if it is present, we can translate: 'Abiathar
(the high-priest)', meaning, Abiathar (who afterwards became) the (famous) high-priest, rather as we could write:
'Prince Albert (the Prince Consort)' even before he obtained
the title by which he became known to history.

27, 28. Verse 27 is omitted by Matthew and Luke but sums up the
lesson. Yet how does 28 ('*therefore* the *Son of Man* is Lord
also of the Sabbath') follow from the above? Possibly, our
Lord meant that His authority extended over the man-made

22

rules about the Sabbath itself; but since 'the Son of Man' was not yet, on our Lord's lips, obviously identical with 'I', it may have sounded to His listeners that He meant merely that 'man is master even of the Sabbath—man can, when necessity compels, dispense from the rules that man has made'.

CHAPTER THREE

Healing on the Sabbath: 1–6
(Matt. 12: 9–14; Luke 6: 6–11)

1. And he entered again into the synagogue: and there was a man there who had a withered hand.
2. And they watched him whether he would heal on the sabbath days, that they might accuse him.
3. And he said to the man who had the withered hand: Stand up in the midst.
4. And he saith to them: Is it lawful to do good on the sabbath days, or to do evil? To save life, or to destroy? But they held their peace.

---

1. Apparently at Capharnaum (see 1: 21) though the Greek has merely 'a synagogue': the chapter might better have begun with verse 7. 'Who had his hand dried up' suggests that this had lasted for some time, but not from birth. 'They watched him', παρατηρεῖν; to watch (someone) askance—almost 'out of the corner of their eyes'. Τὰ σάββατα, see above: 'on the sabbath'. 'They' means the Pharisees, probably those already mentioned: it was not allowed to give any medical help on the sabbath—not even to pour water on a crushed limb or a wound, save in imminent danger of death.
3. Our Lord insisted on the position being openly recognized.
4. His question is rhetorical rather than logical. He means: 'May one do good on the sabbath-day, or is one forbidden to? To restore a man to life, or must one leave him crippled?' A man whose right hand (Luke) was useless was but half-alive: it would be wrong to leave him so, if one could cure him. But the *form of words*, and the actual event, marked only one instance of His indignation that 'charity' should be so

24

5. And looking round about on them with anger, being grieved for the blindness of their hearts, he saith to the man: Stretch forth thy hand. And he stretched it forth. And his hand was restored unto him.
6. And the Pharisees going out, immediately made a consultation with the Herodians against him, how they might destroy him.

---

sacrificed to formalism. 'Looking round at them' (a vivid word proper to Mark 3: 5, 34; 5: 32; 9: 8; 10: 23; 11: 11—save once in Luke 6: 10, parallel to this passage); we have here a rare example of our Lord's exterior behaviour—He looked round into people's eyes, in anger or sorrow, driving men to look at *Him*, showing what *He* thought, and unveiling what *they* thought. He looks around, and looks straight into the mind of each. He was συνλυπούμενος over the πώρωσις of their hearts. Two difficult words. The former means 'grieving *with*'. With whom? It can well mean an interior grief: He suffered 'with Himself'; but more usually, grieving with another—He was both indignant with them, and sorry for their condition which *ought* to have been painful to them even if it was not. It is possible for a man to suffer from his sense that he is irresponsive to a distress that might have been his—and this is just what the Pharisees were: πώρωσις means, precisely, an insensibility, as, for example, if a bone is broken and then mended, there may be a hardening of the new material which forms the joint, and this feels nothing. Compare Eph. 4: 18, also Rom. 11: 25. Our Lord's heart can have been, not only indignant, but sorry for men who did not realize that they were ill spiritually. Not to have an 'ear for music', or 'an eye for colour', is a pity: but not a fault. To be 'insensitive' to right and wrong is a much greater disability, and as a rule the result of long moral disobedience. Conscience ends by not even stammering: a man can 'talk it down': see Rom. 1: 31.

5. 'Was restored', 'Απεκατεστάθη. A very graphic word: 'was thoroughly restored from its ill state'.
6. The Herodians were not an organized group but, presumably,

Our Lord Beside the Sea: 7–12
(Matt. 12: 15–21; Luke 6: 17–19)

7. But Jesus retired with his disciples to the sea: and a great multitude followed him from Galilee and Judea,

8. And from Jerusalem, and from Idumea, and from beyond the Jordan. And they about Tyre and Sidon, a great multitude, hearing the things which he did, came to him.

9. And he spoke to his disciples that a small ship should wait on him, because of the multitude, lest they should throng him.

10. For he healed many, so that they pressed upon him for to touch him, as many as had evils.

Jews who instead of hating the family of the Herods flattered and influenced Antipas. Since all the preceding incidents had taken place in Galilee which was in the jurisdiction of Antipas, the Judaean Pharisees had to obtain leave as it were to 'extradite' Jesus, if not to execute Him on the spot.

The incidents from 3: 7 to 4: 1 are in a different order in Luke: Mark did not always follow the 'sequence of events' (p. xvii): in fact, in verse 9 our Lord orders a boat to be got ready and then climbs a mountain and various other incidents occur, and the boat reappears only in 4: 1.

7. Read 'and', not 'but'; a full-stop should follow 'a great multitude from Galilee followed Him': then St Mark adds that another multitude came from *outside* Galilee—people came from Judea and even the capital city, Jerusalem, and even Idumea (Edom); this must mean a territory south of Jerusalem, which had been won back by John Hyrcanus: its religion remained, or became Jewish, but the name 'Edom' survived. 'Beyond Jordan' was then known as Peraea. Tyre and Sidon were pagan, but in close connection with Upper Galilee.

9. 'Should wait on him', $\Pi\rho o\sigma\kappa\alpha\rho\tau\epsilon\rho\hat{\eta}$, 'should be at his disposal: firmly attached to his use'. St Mark alone gives the practical reason for this: our Lord did not mean to escape across the water.

26

11. And the unclean spirits, when they saw him, fell down before him: and they cried, saying:

12. Thou art the Son of God. And he strictly charged them that they should not make him known.

The Call of the Twelve: 13–19
(Matt. 10: 2–4; Luke 6: 12–16)

13. And going up into a mountain, he called unto him whom he would himself. And they came to him.

14. And he made that twelve should be with him and that he might send them to preach.

15. And he gave them power to heal sicknesses and to cast out devils.

16. And to Simon he gave the name Peter.

---

10. 'Evils' (*Μάστιξ*) need not mean a punishment: we too can speak of an epidemic, etc., as a 'scourge'.

11. Here the evil spirits are seen taking the initiative and acting unanimously. Luke 4: 41 seems to regard 'the Son of God' as equivalent to 'Messias' which our Lord does not use of Himself. Observe that He does not *disclaim* the title 'Son of God', but refuses to have it made public, especially when spoken by evil spirits. He keeps to the title 'Son of Man', and lets events gradually make its bearing clear (cf. pp. xix, xx).

13. In Greek, 'the mountain'. St Peter characteristically does not say *which*. He just remembers the mountain to which our Lord in fact climbed and to which He summoned others— they were *His* choice and not their own (cf. John 6: 70; 15: 16; Acts 1: 2). Not: 'they came to Him', but, 'they went away to him' (*ἀπῆλθον*). Whatever association with Him had previously been theirs, this was their definite vocation.

14. The Greek is awkward, but the sense is clear. 'He arranged' that Twelve should be (i) His habitual associates whom He would train to (ii) go and preach in His name.

16–19. St Mark does not say that He gave them additional names *then*—in fact, He had told Simon that he would be called Cephas (i.e. Petros, rock) long ago (John 1: 42) but did not

17. And James the son of Zebedee, and John the brother of James; and he named them Boanerges, which is, The sons of thunder.

18. And Andrew and Philip, and Bartholomew and Matthew, and Thomas and James of Alpheus, and Thaddeus and Simon the Cananean.

---

explain this till the event described in Mark 16: 16. The following names are in the accusative without a governing verb, but St Mark patently expects us to understand that our Lord *called* these men. John and James were presumably 'nicknamed' 'Sons of the Thunderbolt' because of their asking if they should bring down fire from heaven and destroy the village which would not receive our Lord (Luke 9: 54). Andrew is the brother of Simon but is coupled with Philip in Acts 1: 13 and cf. John 12: 22. These are the only two with Greek names: they both came from Bethsaida (John 1: 44). There is an old but not universal tradition that Bar-Tholomew (Son of Tholomai) is the same as Nathanael (John 1: 45). Matthew is the same as Levi (2: 14); James, 'son of Alphaeus,' to distinguish him from the son of Zebedee; if Alphaeus is the same as Klopas (John 19: 25) he must have taken a Greek name, e.g. Kleopatros, abbreviated into Kleopas which Aramaic would have pronounced Klopa: Thomas was nicknamed 'the twin' (John 19: 16, etc.): it is not known whose twin he was. Thaddeus is the same as Jude (Matt. 10: 3): some MSS. write Lebbaeus instead. Simon Kananaeus becomes translated by St Luke (6: 15 and Acts 1: 13) 'Zelotes', 'the zealous'. The Zelots were a party that had long been seditious, but had not yet become criminally fanatic as they did later, specially under the emperor Titus: one could be 'zealous' without belonging to any such party (cf. Acts 21: 20; Gal. 1: 14) and the name here may well have been a sort of nickname indicating his temperament. Judas 'Iskarioth' means 'Man from Qirioth'; but this is a Hebrew form whereas Aramaic was then talked: however, Hebrew names were often preserved unchanged in educated Aramaic.

19. And Judas Iscariot, who also betrayed him.

Our Lord's Relatives: 20–21

20. And they come to a house: and the multitude cometh together again, so that they could not so much as eat bread.
21. And when his friends had heard of it, they went out to lay hold on him. For they said: He is become mad.

His father was Simon (John 6: 71; 12: 26): Kerioth was a town in Judea; if indeed he came thence, he was the only Judean apostle. Our Lord would not have called him had he not possessed good qualities which, in spite of all, he afterwards allowed to become corrupted.

21. Who were 'his friends', οἱ παρ' αὐτοῦ? Perhaps people in Capharnaum who were on the whole favourable to our Lord, but thought that there was far too much popular excitement. The words are used as 'companions in arms', etc., in 1 Maccab. 9: 44 and often. But it is hard to suppose that 'men of his party', or 'on his side' could be used *not* including the Twelve who certainly were not among those who tried to 'lay hold of him'. It has been suggested that the house belonged to friends or relatives of our Lord; that He had not been able to enter it because of the crowds, and that they came out to pull Him into the house and enable Him to eat. But we never heard of our Lord's relatives living at Capharnaum. So if 'His people' were actually His relatives from Nazareth, we must assume that some time must have passed for the news of the popular enthusiasm to reach them, and for them to come from Nazareth. Hence verse 21 will mean: 'His friends came out to lay hold of Him, *for people were saying . . .*'. This change of subject is exactly like that in 2: 18, and cf. 2: 30. What follows is, then, not the opinion of His relatives, but what they heard was being said. And what was this? That He was 'out of himself', certainly not (as in the Vg.) that 'he has gone mad'. Ἐξέστη in Mark means that one is 'lost' (as we ourselves say) in surprise, admiration or enthusiasm. Compare also

29

Satan's Kingdom: 22–30
(Matt. 12: 24; Luke 11: 15)

22. And the scribes who were come down from Jerusalem, said: He hath Beelzebub, and by the prince of devils he casteth out devils.

5: 42; Luke 8: 56; Acts 10: 44; 2 Cor. 5: 13. We think, then, that it was felt at Capharnaum that popular excitement was getting out of hand and that our Lord Himself was being swept away by it, and that news of this reached Nazareth and caused His relatives to start for Capharnaum, and that their arrival is announced in verses 31 and following. The discussions with the Scribes may have occurred between the information reaching Nazareth and the actual arrival of the relatives. It does not at all follow that 'the friends', οἱ παρ' αὐτοῦ, are the *same* as the relatives of verse 31. We can distinguish between the 'well-wishers' or 'sympathizers' and the relatives themselves.

22. Perhaps St Mark is showing the different 'reactions' to our Lord's preaching—the enthusiasm of the crowds, the anxiety (and perhaps scepticism) of His 'people', the bitter attacks of the Jerusalem Scribes. The sequence of events seems more natural in Matthew (12: 22–24). They said: 'He has (i.e. is possessed by) Beelzebub', and: 'it is by means of the ruler of the devils that he casts the devils out'. Baal-Zebub was the god of Akkaron (Ekron) and the name means 'Lord of flies', but the Greek manuscripts usually write *Beel-Zebul*. Now Zebul means 'dung' or 'dunghill', and this change of a letter was not rare among the Hebrews if they wanted e.g. to insult a false god. But why was this god originally called 'lord of flies'? Possibly because flies polluted sacrifices. But why, when King Ochozias was wounded owing to falling from his window, did he send to *this* god for help (4 Kings 1: 2 and following verses)? Possibly his wounds were badly 'dressed' or not at all, and were clustered over by flies, as we have often seen in the East, owing (we presume)

23. And after he had called them together, he said to them in parables: How can Satan cast out Satan?

24. And if a kingdom be divided against itself, that kingdom cannot stand.

25. And if a house be divided against itself, that house cannot stand.

26. And if Satan be risen up against himself, he is divided and cannot stand, but hath an end.

27. No man can enter into the house of a strong man and rob him of his goods, unless he first bind the strong man: and then shall he plunder his house.

---

to the Mohammedan fatalism, which interfered with flies, etc., being brushed away. But even so, why did this local god become the ruler or captain, ἄρχων, of devils? It is suggested that in Aramaic an almost identical word meant 'enemy', so that Baal-Zebub was thought of as the Enemy in chief.

23. 'In parables', i.e. by comparisons. 'Satan', *the* Adversary, was in commoner use than Beelzebub: our Lord's argument is: 'if "devils", as you admit, are evil spirits, and Satan, the chief of evil spirits, expels such spirits, his reign is at an end.' No kingdom, thus divided within itself, can survive: St Luke pictures the result of such a civil war: house will fall on house. St Mark seems to think of 'house' rather as a family divided within itself than as a material house. Anyhow, the point would be that anything divided against itself cannot last, but 'is finished'.

27. Our Lord now goes further. He brushes aside the idea that He casts out devils by means of the devil, but says that if a man wishes to get the better of a strong man, he must first tie the strong man up, and then he can pillage his house. He leaves us to understand that it is *He* who can first bind Satan, and then gain control of all that Satan has in his possession. We must not turn the parables into an allegory and invent separate meanings for 'house', 'possessions', etc.; the only meaning is that He, our Lord, is stronger than Satan, can conquer him, and can deliver those whom he holds captive.

31

28. Amen I say to you that all sins shall be forgiven unto the sons of men, and the blasphemies wherewith they shall blaspheme:

29. But he that shall blaspheme against the Holy Ghost shall never have forgiveness, but shall be guilty of an everlasting sin.

30. Because they said: He hath an unclean spirit.

28–30. '*Amen*', 'assuredly', used here for the first time in Mark, emphasizes the solemnity of what follows. 'Sons of men' here means simply 'men' (cf. p. xx). This 'logion' has always been a difficulty, partly because St Matthew and St Luke report it in a different form (see below). We know that there is no limit to the mercy of God and that a sincere act of contrition will win His forgiveness for any sin, however grave. Here our Lord says that everything shall be pardoned to men, the sins and the blasphemies—as many as they may be—but whoever blasphemes against the Holy Ghost has no pardon for ever, but is ἔνοχος, responsible, for an everlasting sin (for they were saying: 'He has an impure spirit'). St Matthew (12: 31–32) writes: 'Every sin and blasphemy shall be forgiven men, but the blasphemy of the Spirit shall not be forgiven. And whosoever shall speak a word against the Son of Man, it shall be forgiven him, but he that shall speak against the Holy Ghost, it shall not be forgiven him, neither in this world nor in the world to come.' St Luke (12: 10) writes: 'And whosoever speaketh a word against the Son of Man, it shall be forgiven him: but to him who shall blaspheme against the Holy Ghost it shall not be forgiven.' From Matthew and Luke it is clear that 'the Son of Man' means our Lord, and that it might be possible to fail to recognize, in His humble humanity, the Son of God: insults due to ignorance—even curses spoken in anger—could win forgiveness; all three evangelists make it sufficiently clear that an obstinate refusal to recognize works such as our Lord was doing as divine, but rather to assign them to the devil, indicates a 'hardening of the heart' so absolute that repentance could not be hoped for. St Thomas says that a sin may be

His Mother and Brethren arrive: 31–35
(Matt. 12: 46–50; Luke 8: 19–21)

31. And his mother and his brethren came and, standing without, sent unto him, calling him.

32. And the multitude sat about him. And they say to him: Behold thy mother and thy brethren without seek for thee.

33. And answering them, he said: Who is my mother and my brethren?

---

unforgivable because of final impenitence; or when there are no extenuating circumstances (weakness; ignorance); or when it has destroyed the roots of repentance in the soul, somewhat as the body may lose the very power of getting better. If this is possible, the Church, when praying for such souls, is asking clearly for a miracle of grace. But why should such sin be called against the Holy Ghost in particular? The Holy Spirit is always interceding within the soul (Rom. 8: 26, 27) and if the soul is obdurate to that voice, it kills the very origin of its cure.

31. It is almost certain that these new arrivals are those who were described as starting in verse 21. Our Lady may have decided to come too, because she was (naturally) anxious about what was being said concerning her Son, and quite probably because she felt she might prevent the others from being too rough (for they did not yet believe in Him). Why was St Joseph absent? Either (more probably) because he had died; or possibly because he could not leave his house and work. The question and answer here recorded show that our Lord first put into practice what He was later to preach—that spiritual claims take precedence over those of flesh and blood however dear. He was to say: 'He that loveth father or mother—son or daughter—*more than me*, is not worthy of me' (Matt. 10: 37; cf. Luke 12: 51–53; 14: 25–27; 17: 33). He therefore Himself put His apostolate first, even though it involved a great renunciation: nor was there to be a sort of 'royal family' who should try to control one another. *The*

34. And looking round about on them who sat about him, he saith: Behold my mother and my brethren.

35. For whosoever shall do the will of God, he is my brother and my sister and mother.

Brethren of our Lord. No argument can be based on the Greek word ἀδελφός, since alike the words ἀδελφός and *frater* in Greek and Latin were used strictly to mean the son of the same parents, or, more loosely, to mean 'kindred', or, quite loosely, 'associates'. But in Hebrew and Aramaic the word thus translated is employed in the sense of anyone closely allied by blood—nephew (e.g. Gen. 19: 8; 14: 14, 16; 29: 16), or cousin (1 Par. 22: 21, 22; Lev. 10: 4). Moreover, those languages had no word for 'cousin': one would have to say: 'the son of my father's brother' or 'of my mother's sister', and as a matter of fact, the word 'brother' was normally used for 'cousin'. In the New Testament, our Lord's 'brethren' are never called sons of Mary: when He was twelve, He was clearly an only son (Luke 2: 41 ff.): in Mark 6: 3, the people of Nazareth ask: 'Is not this *the* son of Mary and brother of James and Joses and Jude and Simon?' But in 15: 40 James and Joses (same spelling, whereas St Matthew uses 'Joseph') are sons of a different Mary. The other James was a son of Alphaeus. We are then right in regarding the two first-named as kinsmen, not sons of our Lady, nor yet therefore were the two who follow them sons of hers.

CHAPTER FOUR

The Parables: The Sower: 1–9
(Matt. 13: 1–9; Luke 8: 4–8)

1. And again he began to teach by the sea side. And a great multitude was gathered together unto him, so that he went up into a ship and sat in the sea: and all the multitude was upon the land by the sea side.
2. And he taught them many things in parables and said unto them in his doctrine:
3. Hear ye: Behold, the sower went out to sow.
4. And whilst he sowed, some fell by the way side: and the birds of the air came and ate it up.
5. And other some fell upon stony ground, where it had not much earth: and it shot up immediately, because it had no depth of earth.
6. And when the sun was risen, it was scorched: and because it had no root, it withered away.

---

1. 'A great multitude was gathered together' (συνάγεται πλεῖστος) shows that the crowd was larger than ever: He 'sat', as a teacher would; or because it would be harder to stand even in an anchored boat.
2. 'He began to teach them many things, in parables, in His (own way of) teaching.' Parables were mentioned in 3: 23; but here St Mark wishes to emphasize, we think, this particular *method*: 'He taught them many things in his teaching' would be very clumsy: our Lord is shown as beginning to use a special way of setting forth His doctrine.
4. Palestinian paths were not defined by, e.g., hedges, but were tracks beaten even across a field by reapers, etc. Small birds are still seen following a sower and catching grain even before it reaches the ground.

7. And some fell among thorns: and the thorns grew up and choked it. And it yielded no fruit.

8. And some fell among good ground and brought forth fruit that grew up and increased and yielded, one thirty, another sixty, and another a hundred.

9. And he said: He that hath ears to hear, let him hear.

5, 6. St Luke, however, pictures it as on the ground and trodden on. Palestine was a very stony land. A tale was told that an angel flying over it with a sack of innumerable stones let the sack split and all the stones fell out: and a proverb said that even a goat could not get his nose down between the stones. Grain could begin to shoot even in one night, especially owing to the south-east winds which usually follow the rains needed for sowing: then the blazing sun could easily shrivel the tender shoots, since the thin soil held no moisture.

7. Agriculture may be improving today: but even quite recently men were too lazy to uproot brambles, etc., but lopped them off or burnt them. Even so, they grow with extreme rapidity and being far tougher than the soft wheat they choke it.

8. These figures are a characteristic oriental exaggeration and can even have been spoken by our Lord with a smile and greeted by a laugh. In Gen. 26: 12, a 'hundredfold' increase is mentioned, as also in Pliny; modern Arabs speak in the same way of 40- or 50-fold, whereas they are said normally to get about 3-fold increase on their sowing: not long ago the splendid work of the Trappists did not get more than 13-fold on their sowing of wheat or barley.

9. 'He who has ears that *can* hear—let him use them!' Idols 'have ears, but hear not'. Men too can shut their ears, or be too obtuse to understand what they hear, just as they can have eyes that cannot (or will not) 'see' what they are looking at. We ourselves say: 'There are none so blind as those who won't see.' Anyhow, our Lord makes it clear that He is urging His hearers to discover the *point* of the 'parable' He relates.

Explanation of this Parable: 10-20
(Matt. 13: 10-15; Luke 8: 9-10)

10. And when he was alone, the twelve that were with him asked him
the parable.

11. And he said to them: To you it is given to know the mystery of the
kingdom of God: but to them that are without, all things are done in
parables:

---

10. St Mark (it was early said; see p. xii) did not write 'in the
order in which things happened'. The explanation of this
parable may well have occurred later (as in Luke) when they
crossed the lake in the evening (4: 35) and were 'in private'
and the disciples asked for the explanation of the parables
(*plural*) which apparently our Lord related while still in the
ship: the explanation occurred when He was 'alone' with the
Twelve (10). The point is, that our Lord is entering on the
second part of His teaching, which concerned what He meant
by the 'Kingdom of God', and that He did this *gradually*,
according as His hearers could understand (note the very
important verse 33). He did not reject the Jewish aspiration
for *a* Kingdom of God, but knew that His hearers would take
this to mean the eviction of all pagans from Palestine, and the
enthronement of a king powerful militarily and financially in
Jerusalem.

11. His meaning was a 'mystery', a word used by the evangelists
only here and in parallel passages, though in a somewhat
different sense by St Paul (21 times) and in the Apocalypse
(4 times). Here it means something beyond the obvious meaning of the words, and our Lord challenges His hearers to think
what it may be. Those 'outside' has not at all the 'taste' of
our word 'outsiders', but simply means those who cannot at
present assimilate the full spiritual doctrine 'hinted at' by the
parables.

12. That seeing they may see and not perceive; and hearing they may hear and not understand: lest at any time they should be converted and their sins should be forgiven them.

13. And he saith to them: Are you ignorant of this parable? And how shall you know all parables?

14. He that soweth, soweth the word.

15. And these are they by the way side, where the word is sown, and as soon as they have heard, immediately Satan cometh and taketh away the word that was sown in their hearts.

---

12. These words, which are an allusion to Isaias 6: 9, 10, sound as if our Lord spoke in 'parables' *in order that* He should not be understood. It would be out of place to comment on the bitterly ironic words of the prophet: the only point here is that our Lord means that He cannot say everything all at once, because His hearers were incapable of 'taking in' the essence of His spiritual teaching. So 'everything' had to be insinuated to them by means of 'parables'—such as they liked, and no doubt He did too. The parallels (especially John 12: 39 ff.; and cf. Acts 27: 25 ff.) leave no doubt but that for some at least of our Lord's hearers the obscurity of His doctrine was a punishment. This was specially true for those who had seen His miracles and still refused to follow Him. They had hardened their hearts from the outset, and God will not force our free-wills into 'hearing' and obeying Him.

13. This verse implies that our Lord has already told the disciples several parables—'all the parables'—or else He says with gentle irony: 'If you don't understand this (relatively simple) parable, how will you understand all the parables (that I am going to speak)?' The parable of the Sower *is* a 'parable', though almost an allegory in which every detail corresponds with some other item which it symbolizes. You will notice, here, that the 'seed' is the 'word', i.e. our Lord's *doctrine*. But in the explanation, the seed is often those who hear the doctrine. In fact, our Lord is thinking *both* of the doctrine *and* of those who hear it and in various ways assimilate it or fail

16. And these likewise are they that are sown on the stony ground: they who, when they have heard the word, immediately receive it with joy.

17. And they have no root in themselves, but are only for a time: and then when tribulation and persecution ariseth for the word they are presently scandalized.

18. And others there are who are sown among thorns: these are they that hear the word,

19. And the cares of the world and the deceitfulness of riches and the lusts after other things entering in choke the word: and it is made fruitless.

20. And these are they who are sown upon the good ground: they who hear the word and receive it and yield fruit, the one thirty, another sixty, and another a hundred.

The Candle: 'Attend to the Light!': 21-23
(Matt. 5: 15, 16)

21. And he said to them: Doth a candle come in to be put under a bushel or under a bed, and not to be set on a candlestick?

---

to do so. In verse 15, He says: 'These are they alongside of the way where the word is sown': the distinction is clear. They are 'hard of heart', like stony ground, and Satan, the 'Adversary', makes them reject or fail to attend to what they have heard. How many sermons fall on 'deaf ears' which have none the less heard every spoken word! It has 'meant nothing to them'.

16, 17. Others are upon ground where the soil is shallow; i.e. they have no perseverance, and even if they are attracted by Christ's doctrine, give in when difficulties arise. 'To be scandalized' (σκανδαλίζεσθαι) means to be tripped up, or, to be caught in a snare.

18, 19. Worldly cares, the *cheat* of riches, and greed of every sort 'make their way in' and choke the Word.

20. The 'thirty-fold', etc., mean simply that not even those who accept the Word are equally true to it in life.

39

22. For there is nothing hid which shall not be made manifest: neither was it made secret but that it may come abroad.

23. If any man have ears to hear, let him hear.

Attention is rewarded: 24, 25

(Matt. 13: 12; 25: 29; Luke 6: 38; 19: 26)

24. And he said to them: Take heed what you hear. In what measure you shall mete it shall be measured to you again: and more shall be given to you.

25. For he that hath, to him shall be given: and he that hath not, that also which he hath shall be taken away from him.

---

21. The point is that if our Lord speaks 'obscurely', in 'parables', it is only for a time. Gradually, His full meaning will be understood. The 'little lamp' arrives (i.e. is brought), not to be put under a *modius*, a large pot such as grain could be kept in, though it could also be used to shield a small light which was meant to remain alight till next day—nor, certainly, under a table (not 'bed') but is normally meant to be put on a tall lamp-stand so as to give light to a whole room. So too the parables would in due course be explained. Our Lord taught no 'secret doctrine'.

24. A new recommendation to pay attention to, reflect on, what they hear, for according to the trouble you take, will be your reward, and indeed a generous one! Such seems to be the sense here, though in Matt. 7: 2 and Luke 6: 38, the words are applied to giving generously to one's *neighbour*. Possibly this was a proverb, used more than once by our Lord in different

25. ways; so too 25: the original proverb may have been sarcastic —it is the rich to whom one gives further gifts: the poor are made still poorer. Here our Lord teaches that if one attends to His words, one will receive grace, and, indeed, grace to understand even better. But if one pays little or no attention, one risks losing even what grace one was given at first—for God is always the first to give!

The Grain germinating of itself: 26–29

26. And he said: So is the kingdom of God, as if a man should cast seed into the earth,

27. And should sleep and rise, night and day, and the seed should spring and grow up whilst he knoweth not.

28. For the earth of itself bringeth forth fruit, first the blade, then the ear, afterwards the full corn in the ear.

29. And when the fruit is brought forth, immediately he putteth in the sickle, because the harvest is come.

The Mustard Seed: 30–34

(Matt. 13: 31–32; Luke 13: 18–19)

30. And he said: To what shall we liken the kingdom of God? Or to what parable shall we compare it?

---

26. This lovely little parable is only in Mark. We must not force its details into separate spiritual meanings. The sower does what he can, and leaves the rest to God. One morning he wakes up, and finds the red earth shimmering with the delicate new green. Then the seed grows, ripens, and is fit for the harvest. It is assumed that the soil is good soil, so that the grain *can* grow. Spiritually, of course, nothing is automatic— though in the earth, the grain, left to the action of sun and rain, develops without the sower's needing, or being able, to give it further attention. More spiritually, God gives grace to a good heart, and there will be no resistance: the heavenly life develops in such a soil till it is ready for heaven itself. Or, again, our Lord inaugurates the Church, disappears at His ascension, and then, without any new, additional intervention, the Church will develop till the Day on which He will come again and make His final harvesting. 'Is come' (παρέστηκε), when the grain is ready for it. It is not meant that men need not do anything to arrive at their spiritual maturity but that the action of Grace is beyond human calculation (cf. John 3: 8).

31. It is as a grain of mustard seed: which when it is sown in the earth is less than all the seeds that are in the earth:

32. And when it is sown, it groweth up and becometh greater than all herbs and shooteth out great branches, so that the birds of the air may dwell under the shadow thereof.

33. And with many such parables, he spoke to them the word, according as they were able to hear.

34. And without parable he did not speak unto them: but apart, he explained all things to his disciples.

---

30. More accurately: 'In what parable shall we place it?' (i.e. describe it).

31. Mustard-seed was proverbially small: but it could grow up (Matt. 13: 32) into a regular 'tree' with bark round its stem: in Palestine, birds come and peck at the sharp-flavoured seeds.

32. 'Herbs' (λάχανα): 'vegetables': this suggests what St Luke says—it was sown in a garden. The whole point of the parable is that the Kingdom begins from very small beginnings and becomes very great. So with the Visible Church. One may regret that St Mark did not follow this parable, as St Matthew and St Luke do, with that of the Yeast, which describes the invisible interior action of God's grace.

33, 34. St Mark does not profess to have made an exhaustive list of our Lord's parables; he says with 'many parables of this sort used he to teach', adds the explanation—He was adapting Himself to the receptivity of the listeners. Cf. John 16: 12; I Cor. 3: 2. In private, He explained the parables more exactly to His disciples who could understand rather more. But He does not suggest that the ordinary listener should not do his best to discover the spiritual sense of these little stories. In this series of three, we see that the seed is sown: that it does not remain barren but grows: and that it becomes something very great.

A Storm is Stilled: 35–41
(Matt. 8: 23–27: Luke 8: 22–25)

35. And he saith to them that day, when evening was come: Let us pass over to the other side.

36. And sending away the multitude, they take him even as he was in the ship: and there were other ships with him.

37. And there arose a great storm of wind: and the waves beat into the ship, so that the ship was filled.

38. And he was in the hinder part of the ship, sleeping upon a pillow. And they awake him and say to him: Master, doth it not concern thee that we perish?

39. And rising up, he rebuked the wind and said to the sea: Peace. Be still. And the wind ceased: and there was made a great calm.

40. And he said to them: Why are you fearful? Have you not faith yet? And they feared exceedingly.

---

36. 'Just as He was' (ὡς ἦν), i.e. without disembarking, e.g. to fetch food or extra clothes. St Mark alone says that other ships came too, either because their owners did not want to be separated from Jesus, or, because they had to resume their usual night-fishing.

37. Violent storms can rise on this lake, especially when the south-west wind rushes through the mountain gullies. The boat was 'already' (ἤδη) becoming full of water. Thirteen would have been an unusual load.

38. Often there was a bench or even a small cabin aft: here our Lord was sleeping with His head on *the* pillow—St Mark alone mentions this vivid touch: and only here do the evangelists *speak* of our Lord as sleeping. The disciples seem to think that our Lord, even asleep, would know of their plight.

39. Not 'rising up', but 'waking up'. He speaks to the elements as able to hear and obey Him—'Hush! Be silenced!' (cf. 1: 5).

40. 'Have you not *yet* got faith?', i.e. in God's power manifesting itself in Him.

43

41. And they said one to another: Who is this (thinkest thou) that both wind and sea obey him?

---

41. They were utterly awestruck, as men are when confronted with the supernatural. They had faith, but not full faith yet.

CHAPTER FIVE

The Demoniac of Gerasa: 1-20
(Matt. 8: 28-34; Luke 8: 26-39)

1. And they came over the strait of the sea into the country of the Gerasenes.
2. And as he went out of the ship, immediately there met him out of the monuments a man with an unclean spirit,
3. Who had his dwelling in the tombs: and no man now could bind him, not even with chains.
4. For having been often bound with fetters and chains, he had burst the chains and broken the fetters in pieces: and no one could tame him.
5. And he was always day and night in the monuments and in the mountains, crying and cutting himself with stones.

---

1. The Greek has: 'to the opposite coast.' The MSS. hesitate between Gerasens, Gadarenes, and Gergesenes. The actual town of Gerasa was some 30 miles away in Peraea, but its territory may have extended to the lake. There still exists a village called Kursi near a steep declivity, and this is more probably referred to than anywhere else.
2, 3. 'Monuments': μνήμεια and μνήματα both mean 'tombs', doubtless cave-tombs, or cut out of the rock-face. St Matthew speaks of two men, as later (20: 30), of two blind men, when St Mark mentions only one.
4. If there were two, it may be that one was the more violent and that the event concerned him primarily. No one 'any longer' could bind him: he had often been bound with fetters and chains, and had snapped the chains and 'crushed' the fetters (which may have been wooden).

45

6. And seeing Jesus afar off, he ran and adored him.

7. And crying with a loud voice, he said: What have I to do with thee, Jesus the Son of the Most High God? I adjure thee by God that thou torment me not.

8. For he said unto him: Go out of the man, thou unclean spirit.

9. And he asked him: What is thy name? And he saith to him: My name is Legion, for we are many.

10. And he besought him much that he would not drive him away out of the country.

11. And there was there near the mountain a great herd of swine, feeding.

12. And the spirits besought him, saying: Send us into the swine, that we may enter into them.

6, 7. Not 'adored' him, but flung himself down before him, yelling: 'What to me and to thee?' (cf. 1: 25): practically: 'Keep off me!' 'Son of God-most-High' does not mean that he realized our Lord's divinity—in fact, he adjures Him *by* God; and while 'God-most-High' was a divine title not rare in Asiatic pagan cults, it frequently meant the 'God of the Jews'.

8. This shows that our Lord had begun His 'exorcism' before the possessed man thus cried out—or perhaps His very approach was a sort of beginning of purification. St Matthew adds 'before the appointed moment' ($\pi\rho\grave{o}$ $\kappa\alpha\iota\rho o\hat{v}$), as though the evil spirit dwelt for the time being in the man, and was afraid of being sent to his final home in hell.

9. Our Lord now speaks directly to the evil spirit and demands his name: it answers ironically: 'Legion', i.e. very many (the word must not be taken as denoting 5,000 or 6,000, the number of men in a Roman legion as such).

10. This flock of spirits asks, if they are to be evicted from one man, that at least they may not be evicted from the district (cf. Luke 11: 24).

11. The Jews were severely forbidden to breed swine: this was not always obeyed; but in this chiefly pagan region the rule was less likely to be attended to. The devils ask that they may

13. And Jesus immediately gave them leave. And the unclean spirits going out, entered into the swine. And the herd with great violence was carried headlong into the sea, being about two thousand, and were stifled in the sea.

14. And they that fed them fled and told it in the city and in the fields. And they went out to see what was done.

15. And they come to Jesus. And they see him that was troubled with the devil, sitting, clothed, and well in his wits: and they were afraid.

16. And they that had seen it told them, in what manner he had been dealt with who had the devil: and concerning the swine.

17. And they began to pray him that he would depart from their coasts.

18. And when he went up into the ship, he that had been troubled with the devil began to beseech him that he might be with him.

19. And he admitted him not, but saith to him: Go into thy house to thy friends; and tell them how great things the Lord hath done for thee and hath had mercy on thee.

---

be at least allowed to inhabit this herd of impure beasts. Our Lord allows it. The very beasts rush down the cliff and drown themselves.

14-17. The swineherds, terrified, run away, tell what has happened, return with others, find the man dressed, sitting quiet among the disciples, and master of himself. Even more frightened, they beg the Lord to go away.

18. Touchingly, the healed man asks to attach himself to Jesus.

19, 20. He refuses, and tells him to go home and say how the Lord has had mercy upon him. He does so but proceeds to tell his tale in all the 'Decapolis', a vague term, a term comprising various towns on the east of Galilee, chiefly pagan. There are as it were two parts to this story: first, the terrible condition of the poor man and his perfect cure. We notice that our Lord says nothing to him about repenting, so that it is conceivable that he was mad but innocent and that evil spirits find it easier to torment a disordered mind. Abnormal phenomena seem quite often to suggest a mixture of e.g.

20. And he went his way and began to publish in Decapolis how great things Jesus had done for him: and all men wondered.

The Daughter of Jairus: 21-24

(Matt. 9: 18-19; Luke 7: 40-42)

21. And when Jesus had passed again in the ship over the strait, a great multitude assembled together unto him: and he was nigh unto the sea.
22. And there cometh one of the rulers of the synagogue named Jairus: and seeing him, falleth down at his feet.

---

hysteria and the preternatural. The second part is concerned with the destruction of the swine. It is not hinted that the evil spirits *drove* them into the sea—on the contrary, they seem to want to live in them since they can no more find a home in the man. The swine, then, in an instinctive panic due to the approach of something preternatural and evil, take flight and are drowned. Our Lord does not *cause* the demons to scare the swine but does not prevent their doing so, any more than He prevents natural calamities like floods, earthquakes, etc., or moral calamities due in reality to sin, like wars. St Mark does not consider the rights or wrongs of this destruction of property, but our Lord uses the event as a sort of parable in action—'Unclean to the unclean!' (not that swine *are* unclean, but all Jews held them to be so). It can be observed that e.g. dogs or horses often have an instinctive sense that a person approaching them likes or dislikes them or is frightened of them: still more might they be aware of and alarmed by the approach of an evil spirit.

21. As before, 'to the other side', i.e. to Capharnaum. 'Again' would be better placed after 'assembled'.
22. 'One of the chiefs of synagogue' (εἷς τῶν ἀρχισυναγώγων might imply that there were several synagogues at Capharnaum; but more likely Jairus was simply one of the important members of a synagogue (cf. Acts 3: 15; 14: 2).

23. And he besought him much, saying: My daughter is at the point of death. Come, lay thy hand upon her, that she may be safe and may live.

24. And he went with him. And a great multitude followed him: and they thronged him.

The Woman with an Issue of blood: 25–34
(Matt. 9: 20–23; Luke 8: 43–48)

25. And a woman who was under an issue of blood, twelve years,

26. And had suffered many things from many physicians and had spent all that she had; and was nothing the better, but rather the worse,

27. When she had heard of Jesus, came in the crowd behind him and touched his garment.

28. For she said; If I shall touch but his garment, I shall be whole.

29. And forthwith the fountain of her blood was dried up: and she felt in her body that she was healed of the evil.

30. And immediately Jesus knowing in himself the virtue that had proceeded from him, turning to the multitude, said: Who hath touched my garments?

---

23. 'My little daughter' ($\theta\upsilon\gamma\acute{\alpha}\tau\rho\iota o\nu$): 'at the point of death' ($\dot{\epsilon}\sigma\chi\acute{\alpha}\tau\omega\varsigma$ $\ddot{\epsilon}\chi\epsilon\iota$).

25, 26. 'Under', i.e. who had suffered from a constant flow of blood. We learn that even now Easterns often have the habit of summoning as many doctors as possible, thereby not only incurring great expense but involving a patient in often contradictory treatments.

27. Not only was she shy of mentioning her illness publicly, but it implied a legal taint (Lev. 15: 25). She therefore came up behind, convinced that if she touched 'so much as part of His garment' she would be healed: St Matthew and St Luke mention that it was the $\kappa\rho\acute{\alpha}\sigma\pi\epsilon\delta o\nu$ that she touched—a kind of fringe attached to the four corners of a mantle.

29. She felt in her body—definitely contrasted by St Mark with our Lord's 'clearly perceiving within Himself', *not* 'the virtue

31. And his disciples said to him: Thou seest the multitude thronging thee; and sayest thou who hath touched me?

32. And he looked about to see her who had done this.

33. But the woman fearing and trembling, knowing what was done in her, came and fell down before him and told him all the truth.

34. And he said to her: Daughter, thy faith hath made thee whole. Go in peace: and be thou whole of thy disease.

The Daughter of Jairus: 35–43

(Matt. 9: 23–26; Luke 8: 49–56)

35. While he was yet speaking, some come from the ruler of the synagogue's house, saying: Thy daughter is dead. Why dost thou trouble the master any further?

36. But Jesus having heard the word that was spoken, saith to the ruler of the synagogue: Fear not, only believe.

37. And he admitted not any man to follow him, but Peter and James and John the brother of James.

38. And they come to the house of the ruler of the synagogue. And he seeth a tumult; and people weeping and wailing much.

---

that has proceeded from Him', but 'that the (healing) power had proceeded'. There was no magical power in His garment.

31. 'Thronging' (συνθλίβοντα): a strong word; 'crushing you together'.

33, 34. The woman, awestruck by the miracle, and perhaps fearing a reproach from our Lord, trembling told her whole story: our Lord may have emphasized the role played by her faith, and by His own free will, to teach that the mere touching a garment, even His own, would not bring about a miracle.

35. 'Trouble' (σκύλλειν) a word originally meaning to 'tear', but here softened in sense: practically 'worry', which we ourselves can use in a more or less violent sense, e.g. of a dog 'worrying' a rat, or a cat. These messengers understood neither the heart of the father, nor that of our Lord.

36. 'Having heard' (παρακούσας): 'over-hearing', not in its usual sense of pretending not to hear, refusing to hear.

39. And going in, he saith to them: Why make you this ado and weep? The damsel is not dead, but sleepeth.

40. And they laughed him to scorn. But he having put them all out, taketh the father and the mother of the damsel and them that were with him, and entereth in where the damsel was lying.

41. And taking the damsel by the hand, he saith to her: Talitha cumi, which is, being interpreted: Damsel (I say to thee) arise.

42. And immediately the damsel rose up and walked: and she was twelve years old. And they were astonished with a great astonishment.

43. And he charged them strictly that no man should know it; and commanded that something should be given her to eat.

---

38. 'Seeth a tumult' (literally, 'hubbub'), Θεωρεῖ θόρυβον, a strange expression avoided by St Matthew and St Luke. Still, even in classical Greek one could say: κτύπον δέδορκα; 'I see, i.e. perceive, a noise' (Aeschylus). St Mark does not suggest that the lamentations were made by hired mourners: but St Matthew mentions flute-players, which implies not only that the girl was dead (as her father in fact says, Matt. 9: 18) but that there had been time enough to collect these lugubrious personages: still, in an oriental town there were no doubt plenty at hand; and the episode of the woman whom our Lord cured implied a considerable interruption.

39. If our Lord had simply said the child was asleep, there would be no difficulty: but He said: 'She is *not* dead': cf., however, in John 11: 11, He says that Lazarus was asleep though He knew that he was dead, and meant to bring him to life again; and to 'sleep' became at once a normal Christian word for having 'died'. The Evangelists certainly mean us to understand that the child was dead; but our Lord may well have allowed it to be thought that she was only in a sort of coma, else how could He possibly have 'strictly ordered' the witnesses not to tell anyone what had happened (43)? Anyhow, so brief a death could be called *non*-death in the normal sense. Still, they thought she was dead, because they 'laughed him down'—an exact translation of κατεγέλων. The whole episode is related at such length by St Mark, compared with St Matthew and St Luke that it is idle to call him an 'abbreviator': also, he writes with his characteristic simplicity which is all the more vivid because he in no way 'decorates' his story.

CHAPTER SIX

Our Lord is scorned at Nazareth: 1–6
(Matt. 13: 53–58; cf. Luke 4: 16–30)

1. And going out from thence, he went into his own country and his
   disciples followed him.
2. And when the sabbath was come, he began to teach in the synagogue.
   And many hearing him were in admiration at his doctrine, saying:
   How came this man by all these things? And what wisdom is this that
   is given to him, and such mighty works as are wrought by his hands?
3. Is not this the carpenter, the son of Mary, the brother of James and
   Joseph and Jude and Simon? Are not also his sisters here with us?
   And they were scandalized in regard of him.
4. And Jesus said to them: A prophet is not without honour, but in his
   own country and in his own house and among his own kindred.

---

1 St Luke puts together two preachings at Nazareth: St Mark is
  here writing of the second only: so too St Matthew.
2, 3. 'His doctrine' is not in the Greek. The majority were
  astonished by His authoritativeness, no doubt, and by what
  they had *heard* of the 'so great miracles' worked by Him at
  Capharnaum. They, for their part, had known Jesus personally, as a carpenter, son of Mary (it must be clear that St
  Joseph by now was dead); and His kinsfolk were there
  among them. They were 'shocked' by one of themselves,
  with no special education, putting forth such claims and
  winning such a reputation elsewhere. On our Lord's kinsfolk,
  see p. 34.
4. There were other proverbs not unlike ours—'familiarity
  breeds contempt': the Nazarenes thought they knew our

53

5. And he could not do any miracles there, only that he cured a few that were sick, laying his hands upon them.

6. And he wondered because of their unbelief: and he went through the villages round about teaching.

The Mission of the Twelve: 7–13
(Matt. 9: 35–10: 1; 10: 5–11: 1; Luke 9: 1–6)

7. And he called the twelve and began to send them two and two and gave them power over unclean spirits.

Lord too well to admit that He was in any way 'special'. But we should not take all our Lord's words as though they were scientific statements: cf. 'it cannot be that a prophet should die save only in Jerusalem' (Luke 13: 33).

5. 'He could not.' This implies that the working of a miracle is not mechanical or merely magical. There must be *some* right disposition of heart and mind in the recipient. Cf. the imperfect faith of the epileptic's father, 9: 25.

6. The truth that our Lord was God did not interfere with His experiencing all that was proper to His being truly man. He encountered the fact of their unbelief and marvelled at it: we ourselves can be amazed at the state of mind of people who, we felt quite sure, would take a certain view of things, but did not. None the less, our Lord went on to preach in the surrounding villages.

7. Our Lord begins ($\mathring{\eta}\rho\xi\alpha\tau o$) to train the Apostles to be 'missioners'. He sent them out, each with a companion ($\delta\acute{v}o$ $\delta\acute{v}o$: cf. below; 6: 40: the form of expression is found both in ancient and modern Greek): not only each was to act as a check on the behaviour of the other and to report on it, but a man often needs companionship, lest e.g. he may become despondent, or lest he may make claims that have no 'backing'. Not, 'he gave them power', but 'was giving them power'. He had given it (3: 15), but was continuing to do so (as the results showed).

8. And he commanded them that they should take nothing for the way, but a staff only: no scrip, no bread, nor money in their purse,
9. But to be shod with sandals, and that they should not put on two coats.
10. And he said to them: Wheresoever you shall enter into an house, there abide till you depart from that place.

---

8. On the other hand, He 'ordered them—no bread, no wallet, etc.'. This was a new definite instruction. They were to take only what was strictly needed—no wallet for larger things, no purse (i.e. smaller coins were kept in their girdle); not two 'tunics'. Jews wore a sort of linen under-shirt: an over-dress reaching usually to the knees (richer men might wear also an over-tunic reaching to the feet): the dress would be bound by a girdle—not by a mere cord, like our dressing-gowns, but a wide sash in the folds of which small objects, also money, could be held: and perhaps a square cloth with a fringe (5: 28). Finally, a turban. St Mark says that they were to have sandals and a staff; St Luke (9: 3), says nothing about sandals: St Matthew 10: 10, forbids both staff and shoes (σανδάλια and ὑποδήματα are equivalent). All these passages refer to the same incident, and it is idle to try to 'harmonize' them word for word. We do not know, word for word, what were the inscriptions over the Cross, or even the words used for the institution of the Holy Eucharist. The Evangelists may be following traditions different in detail, but they coincide in the essential —that the Apostles· must in no way seem to be money-making: they must take with them only what was necessary: if they received hospitality, they must not try to exchange for something better (10): if they were refused hospitality, they must 'shake the dust off their feet as a witness about them', i.e. they must not try to 'cadge' hospitality, but show that *that* was not the welcome they were seeking. This echoed the Jewish idea that contact with *any* non-Jewish earth was a pollution. Jews who came back to Palestine had thus to 'shake off' the dust of the pagan world in which they had

11. And whosoever shall not receive you nor hear you: going forth from thence, shake off the dust from your feet for a testimony to them.
12. And going forth they preached that men should do penance:
13. And they cast out many devils and anointed with oil many that were sick and healed them.

---

lived. The act of the Apostles was to symbolize the obstinacy of those who would not receive them, or (therefore) Him who had sent them. In Acts 13: 51, St Paul performs the same symbolical action when leaving the obdurate Jews for the Gentiles.

12, 13. The upshot was that they cast out many demons, and anointed many sick persons with oil and healed them. This 'unction' was clearly not just the use of oil customary among the Jews as a 'softener' e.g. of wounds: but it was a kind of foreshadowing of our sacramental 'Last Anointing'.

Herod the Great married:-

Herod the Great (Matt. 2: 1) married (1) Mariamne, and had a son Aristobulus, who had a son Herod Agrippa I (Acts 12: 14)—whose own son was Herod Agrippa II (Acts 25: 13) who does not concern us here—and a daughter Herodias (Mark 6:

Interlude. *The Martyrdom of St John Baptist*
(i) *King Herod hears of Jesus*: 14–16

(Matt. 14: 1–2; Luke 9: 7–9)

14. And king Herod heard (for his name was made manifest), and he said: John the Baptist is risen again from the dead; and therefore mighty works shew forth themselves in him.

15 And others said: It is Elias. But others said: It is a prophet, as one of the prophets.

---

17). Herod the Great married (2) a second Mariamne, or, more probably, Mariame; they had a son, Herod Philip I (Mark 6: 17), who married Herodias: these had a daughter Salome (Mark 6: 22). Herod the Great married (3) Malthake, whose children were Herod Antipas (Mark 6: 14) and Archelaus (Matt. 2: 22). Finally, Herod the Great married a Cleopatra who had a son Herod Philip II (Luke 3: 2) who married Salome. Enough to say that when Herod the Great died, his kingdom was divided into four parts—Judea was given to Archelaus, who proved a worse monster even than his father, which was why Joseph, returning from Egypt, decided to go back to Galilee (Matt. 2: 22) and why the Jews themselves asked for a Roman 'procurator' instead: Galilee and Peraea were given to Herod Antipas: Ituraea and Trachonitis, east of the lake of Galilee, were given to Herod Philip II, and a district, Abilene, north of Ituraea, was allotted to Lysanias, though not of Herod's family. The last three of these divisions were called 'tetrarchies', 'a fourth-part rule', so to say: Judea was not so called, perhaps because by the time of our Lord it was under separate Roman government; but before that, it may have been too proud to admit that it was merely one with others in a quadruple realm.

14. Herod Antipas was not by nature cruel, but (as we should say) 'impressionable' and easily 'upset'. When our Lord and His works became widely discussed, people said (read ἔλεγον for ἔλεγεν): 'John is resuscitated! That is why, etc.'

16. Which Herod hearing, said: John whom I beheaded, he is risen again from the dead.

The Martyrdom of St John Baptist
(ii) *John is slain and buried*: 17–29

(Matt. 14: 3, 12; Luke 3: 19, 20)

17. For Herod himself had sent and apprehended John and bound him in prison for the sake of Herodias the wife of Philip his brother, because he had married her.

18. For John said to Herod: It is not lawful for thee to have thy brother's wife.

19. Now Herodias laid snares for him and was desirous to put him to death: and could not.

---

15. But others said: 'It is Elias!' See on 9: 11 ff. It was thought by many that Elias was still alive and would reappear before the Messias came. Others said: 'It is a prophet like one of the others'—i.e. there had been no recognized prophets for 400 years: Prophets are beginning again!

16. Herod jumps to the conclusion—because of his guilty conscience—that it must be John whom he had beheaded. St Luke, 9: 9, suggests that he remained a sceptic. 'I beheaded John (so it cannot be he—but who *is* he?).'

17. St Mark (1: 14) has already recorded John's imprisonment. We hold that it was when the herald-Voice was thus silenced that our Lord began His public ministry. The prison is thought to have been within the palace built by Herod the Great, near Machaerus, a town overlooking the east of the Dead Sea.

18. Herodias had already married a son of Herod the Great, who held no official position: having transferred herself to Herod Philip I, she was taken from him by his half-brother, Antipas, without even the technicality of a divorce. John may have denounced this adulterous and incestuous marriage (for both Herod Philip I and Antipas were her uncles) in private; but Herodias will soon have heard of it.

20. For Herod feared John, knowing him to be a just and holy man, and kept him: and when he heard him, did many things. And he heard him willingly.

21. And when a convenient day was come, Herod made a supper for his birthday, for the princes and tribunes and chief men of Galilee.

22. And when the daughter of the same Herodias had come in and had danced and pleased Herod and them that were at table with him, the king said to the damsel: Ask of me what thou wilt, and I will give it thee.

23. And he swore to her: Whatsoever thou shalt ask I will give thee, though it be the half of my kingdom.

24. Who when she was gone out, said to her mother: What shall I ask? But she said: The head of John the Baptist.

25. And when she was come in immediately with haste to the king, she asked, saying: I will that forthwith thou give me in a dish the head of John the Baptist.

---

19. Ἐνεῖχεν αὐτῷ cannot mean 'laid snares for', but 'had it against him', i.e. harboured a grudge against him: possibly 'lay in wait for him': cf. Luke 11: 53.

20. 'Feared' (ἐφοβεῖτο): 'stood in awe of him': 'kept him', almost 'safeguarded him', i.e. against attacks. When he heard him, he was 'much perplexed' (read ἠπόρει, not ἐποίει), for he 'enjoyed listening to him'. Matt. 14: 5 says that he intended to kill him, but was afraid of the people who regarded Jesus as a prophet. In Luke 23: 11 we find Herod hoping to see a miracle worked by our Lord, and mocking Him when He did not. Herod's character was weak; he was easily swayed to and fro.

21. The day was 'convenient' to Herodias: the guests were both civil and military.

22, 23. The offer of the 'half of a kingdom' was almost traditional (so Esther 5: 3: cf. Kings 13: 8; Luke 19: 8).

25. 'Forthwith, with haste'—presumably lest Herod should change his mind.

26. And the king was struck sad. Yet because of his oath and because of them that were with him at table, he would not displease her.

27. But sending an executioner, he commanded that his head should be brought in a dish.

28. And he beheaded him in the prison and brought his head in a dish and gave it to the damsel: and the damsel gave it to her mother.

29. Which his disciples hearing, came and took his body and laid it in a tomb.

The Feeding of Five Thousand: (i) 30–34

(Luke 9: 10; Matt. 12: 14; Luke 9: 11: these speak too of miracles of healing)

30. And the apostles coming together unto Jesus, related to him all things that they had done and taught.

---

26. The King was 'distressed' ($\pi\epsilon\rho\acute{\iota}\lambda\upsilon\pi\sigma$) and *yet* because of his oath sworn before witnesses could not resolve to 'rebuff her' ($\dot{\alpha}\theta\epsilon\tau\hat{\eta}\sigma\alpha\iota$).

27. 'Executioner' ($\sigma\pi\epsilon\kappa\sigma\upsilon\lambda\acute{\alpha}\tau\omega\rho$): St Mark (see p. xiv) often uses Latin words; here, *speculator*: originally one who 'kept an eye' on things and brought news to his employer: then, a member of a body-guard; then, an executioner.

29. John's disciples removed the body and placed it in 'a' grave: St Mark does not say where, nor indeed where the murder took place. The Jewish historian Josephus (d. 101) says that Herod killed John because he feared that the Baptist's popularity and influence might bring about rebellion. Herod may indeed have harboured such a fear, or again, have permitted this reason for his action to have been circulated rather than the horrible true one. When Herod's original wife, daughter of Aretas, king of the Nabataeans, heard of his intention to discard her for Herodias, she fled to her father, who in due course declared war against Antipas and ultimately defeated him. Josephus sees in this a divine punishment for the death of John.

30. St Mark does not say what our Lord was doing while the apostles (a word used only here in Mark save perhaps 3: 14)

31. And he said to them: Come apart into a desert place and rest a little. For there were many coming and going: and they had not so much as time to eat.

32. And going up into a ship, they went into a desert place apart.

33. And they saw them going away: and many knew. And they ran flocking thither on foot from all the cities and were there before them.

34. And Jesus going out saw a great multitude: and he had compassion on them, because they were as sheep not having a shepherd. And he began to teach them many things.

The Feeding of the Five Thousand (ii) 35–44

35. And when the day was now far spent, his disciples came to him saying: This is a desert place and the hour is now past:

---

were away—Peter himself was away, and so could not relate what happened in his absence.

31. As often St Mark first says what happened, and then says why it did (cf. 5: 7 ff.; 6: 17 ff.). A crowd had followed the Twelve, and even when 'going away' would take long to say goodbye and express their thanks.

32. There was no 'desert' place near the lake: 'quiet', or 'lonely'; see verse 45. The point of taking a boat was to ensure freedom

33. from the crowds: if they rowed north-east across the tip of the lake plenty of people could get to where the heavy boat-load was going (it was never out of sight) as soon as it did itself, especially as new and unwearied groups kept joining them as they proceeded. 'Knew': 'understood', i.e., where they were going.

34. The eager but unshepherded multitudes are a great incentive to the apostolate, if but a man's heart be like our Lord's heart. See especially Ezekiel 34 and Mark 14: 27, John 10: 1 ff.

35. 'The day is far spent' ($\H{\omega}\rho\alpha\varsigma$ $\pi o\lambda\lambda\H{\eta}\varsigma$ $\gamma\epsilon\nu o\mu\acute{\epsilon}\nu\eta\varsigma$), need not mean that it was almost dark, and indeed could hardly do so, since the disciples suggest that the people should go off to

36. Send them away, that going into the next villages and towns, they may buy themselves meat to eat.

37. And he answering said to them: Give you them to eat. And they said to him: Let us go and buy bread for two hundred pence, and we will give them to eat.

38. And he saith to them: How many loaves have you? Go and see. And when they knew, they say: Five, and two fishes.

39. And he commanded them that they should make them all sit down by companies upon the green grass.

40. And they sat down in ranks, by hundreds and by fifties.

41. And when he had taken the five loaves and the two fishes: looking up to heaven, he blessed and broke the loaves, and gave to his disciples to set before them. And the two fishes he divided among them all.

---

neighbouring villages and towns and buy food. It was late so far as a midday meal went.

37. The disciples reply to our Lord's bewildering order almost ironically: 'Are we to go and *buy* food (ἀγοράσωμεν), and so feed them?' A *denarius* was a day's wage, and the current silver coin (Jewish rulers were allowed to make only copper coins): even 200 such coins would not have bought enough bread for all!

38. Our Lord says: 'How many loaves have you got? Go! look!'

39. He made them all sit down, 'by groups' (cf. 40) 'on the green grass'. Not only is grass in Palestine scorched brown by the end of May, but it is true to St Mark's style to add this vivid detail: in fact

40. they were arranged not only in groups (συμπόσια συμπόσια) but in rectangles, like 'flower-beds' (πρασιαὶ πρασιαί).

41. In the Consecration at Mass, *elevatis oculis in caelum*, not found in the scriptural account of the institution of the Holy Eucharist, are words probably due to a memory of this passage. It seems that our Lord first broke (κατέκλασεν) and then kept handing out (ἐδίδου) the food to the apostles: it was not multiplied in their hands.

42. And they all did eat and had their fill.

43. And they took up the leavings, twelve full baskets of fragments and of the fishes.

44. And they that did eat were five thousand men.

Our Lord upon the Waters: 45-52
(Matt. 14: 22-23; John 6: 16-21)

45. And immediately he obliged his disciples to go up into the ship, that they might go before him over the water to Bethsaida, whilst he dismissed the people.

46. And when he had dismissed them, he went up to the mountain to pray.

---

44. St Matthew says that the 5,000 were exclusive of women and children. The event recalls the miracle worked by Eliseus (2 Kings 4: 42-44) who fed 100 persons with 20 barley loaves, but there was bread left over. The word used for 'basket' here is κόφινος: see on 8: 8.

45. Our Lord's plan that the disciples should 'rest' had already been defeated; but since St John says (6: 14, 15) that the people, excited by so 'Messianic' a miracle, wished to make Him king, the presence of the disciples might have made things still more difficult. He 'compelled' them to take ship and to row 'over the water' (εἰς τὸ πέραν), which must mean the west coast; πρός can hardly mean 'to Bethsaida', which was in the territory of Herod Philip, Galilee being wholly to the west of Jordan and the Lake. Now it is true that Philip had 'developed' the township of Bethsaida and added to it the name 'Julias', in honour of Augustus's daughter Julia. It is possible that the old and new Bethsaidas were on either side of the entry of Jordan into the lake; but it seems simpler to take πρός as meaning 'facing', or 'opposite to' the town.

46. Our Lord, then, having persuaded the crowds to disperse, went up into the mountain to pray, yet even so, did not forget His friends, for from that height He could actually see

47. And when it was late, the ship was in the midst of the sea, and himself alone on the land.

48. And seeing them labouring in rowing (for the wind was against them) and about the fourth watch of the night, he cometh to them, walking upon the sea: and he would have passed by them.

49. But they, seeing him walking upon the sea, thought it was an apparition: and they cried out.

50. For they all saw him and were troubled. And immediately he spoke with them and said to them: Have a good heart. It is I. Fear ye not.

51. And he went up to them into the ship, and the wind ceased. And they were far more astonished within themselves.

52. For they understood not concerning the loaves: for their heart was blinded.

---

the boat even some miles from the shore, especially as it was Paschal-time and the moon would soon be full. St John (6: 19) says they had gone 25 or 30 furlongs.

48. They were struggling at the oar (literally 'tormented in their rowing')—not that there was a storm, but because the wind was against them—i.e. blowing from the north-west, as it often does because of the formation of the mountains there. The time was the fourth watch, i.e. from 3 a.m. onwards. This was the Roman military way of counting the hours, which had passed too into civil usage. Our Lord came to them walking on the sea; and St Mark emphasizes that they

49, 50. all saw Him and were terrified because they thought He was a ghost. But he adds the strange detail that our Lord 'made as though to pass by them' ($\mathring{\eta}\theta\epsilon\lambda\epsilon$ $\pi\alpha\rho\epsilon\lambda\theta\epsilon\hat{\iota}\nu$); not 'to go ahead of them', but simply to disregard them. We may surmise that He wished to put their faith in Him yet again to the test; but even after He had entered the ship, they

51. were not so much uttering cries of terror, as stunned (a paradox? 'out of themselves within themselves'): literally, 'dumbfounded'.

52. For 'they had not understood about the loaves, for their heart was numbed'; 'heart' means 'power of understanding': it is

64

In Gennesareth: 53–56

(Matt. 14: 34, 36)

53. And when they had passed over, they came into the land of Genesareth and set to the shore.

54. And when they were gone out of the ship, immediately they knew
him:

55. And running through that whole country, they began to carry about
in beds those that were sick, where they heard he was.

56. And whithersoever he entered, into towns or into villages or cities,
they laid the sick in the streets and besought him that they might
touch but the hem of his garment. And as many as touched him were
made whole.

---

quite possible that an event may be so extraordinary as to leave
a witness 'unable to grasp it' or even to believe it really
happened.

54. It is certain that the Lake and the plain through which Jordan
ran were called *Gennesar*: it is probable that *Genesareth* was
the name of a village or port.

55, 56. Read: 'When they had disembarked, forthwith those who
recognized Him began to hasten', etc. 'Streets': ἄγοραι
cannot mean streets, nor market-places, but any open space,
e.g. a courtyard. 'Hem', rather, 'fringe', see Luke 7: 45; and
Mark 5: 27. 'Touched': rather, 'took hold of': cf. John 20:
17.

CHAPTER SEVEN

The Law of God and Traditions of Men: (i) 1–8

(Matt. 15: 1–8)

1. And there assembled together unto him the Pharisees and some of the scribes, coming from Jerusalem.
2. And when they had seen some of his disciples eat bread with common, that is, with unwashed hands, they found fault.
3. For the Pharisees and all the Jews eat not without often washing their hands, holding the tradition of the ancients.
4. And when they come from the market, unless they be washed, they eat not: and many other things there are that have been delivered to

---

1. That is, the local Pharisees, and a group of Scribes arriving from Jerusalem.
2. 'Common', (κοινόν), i.e. anything non-sacred. 'Profane' meant much the same. *Odi profanum vulgus et arceo*: Horace meant 'the common crowd' (Odes, iii, 1, 1). The word did not mean 'impure' till the 'puritan' Jews (as we might say) had ended by regarding anything not 'ceremonially' sacred as somehow morally 'impure'. St Mark, writing for Romans, feels he must explain this; St Matthew, writing primarily for Jews, does not feel he needs to.
3. 'Often'. This translates πυκνά, which is an easier MS. alteration of the difficult word πυγμῇ, which should mean 'with (clenched) fist'. The point is that the Jews, before eating, washed the tips of their fingers: before certain ceremonial meals, the whole fingers: when washing in the Temple, the whole hand, up to the wrist. To make sure of finding 'pure' water, some Rabbis said you must go four miles.

them to observe, the washings of cups and of pots and of brazen vessels and of beds.

5. And the Pharisees and scribes asked him: Why do not thy disciples walk according to the tradition of the ancients, but they eat bread with common hands?

6. But he answering, said to them: Well did Isaias prophesy of you hypocrites, as it is written: *This people honoureth me with their lips, but their heart is far from me.*

7. *And in vain do they worship me, teaching doctrines and precepts of men.*

---

4. There are two MS. versions: βαπτίζωνται and ραντίσωνται: the latter means that if you had been to market, you must 'sprinkle' your hands, lest you might have touched something 'unclean': if you were sure you had, you must take a complete bath. The principle applied not only to persons, but to things. Thus milk might have been mixed with 'unclean' ingredients, or settled on by e.g. flies. St Mark does not mention this, but only 'receptacles'—cups, pots (ξέσται is from the Latin *sextarius* and contained about a pint): 'couches', i.e. what men reclined upon while eating, are not in all MSS.: these, anyhow, can have been only 'sprinkled', not soaked: χαλκία means dishes of bronze or other metals.

5. 'Walk', i.e. behave. Our Lord, as often, does not merely defend Himself (and here, His disciples) but attacks His critics.

6. 'Well' (καλῶς) means 'Isaias was *quite right* in what he said. . . .' The reference is to Isaias 29: 13: but our Lord adapts what the prophet said to the actual situation: in the Hebrew we read, 'This people approaches me with its mouth and with its lips honoureth me, but its heart is far distant from me', and in the LXX (which St Mark follows) the prophet continues: 'and in vain do they worship me, teaching commands and doctrines of men'. The Hebrew therefore says that worship in which the heart is not involved is but a human cult: Our Lord, in Mark, says that the *doctrine taught by the scribes* is but a human invention.

8. For leaving the commandment of God, you hold the tradition of men, the washing of pots and of cups: and many other things you do like to these.

The Law of God and Traditions of Men: (ii) 9–13
(Matt. 15: 3–6)

9. And he said to them: Well do you make void the commandment of God, that you may keep your own tradition.

10. For Moses said: *Honour thy father and thy mother*. And *He that shall curse father or mother, dying let him die*.

11. But you say: If a man shall say to his father or mother, Corban (which is a gift) whatsoever is from me shall profit thee.

12. And further you suffer him not to do any thing for his father or mother,

13. Making void the word of God by your own tradition, which you have given forth. And many other such like things you do.

---

9. 'Well' (καλῶς), here is colloquial Greek, but not slang, as though we should say 'properly', meaning 'thoroughly'. 'Well indeed do you reduce the commandments of God to nothing, all for the sake of your own tradition!'

11. The syntax, not the meaning, is difficult: our translation is unintelligible. *Korban* means a gift, especially a gift given, or promised, to God. One could not then give it to anyone else. If, then, one's parents had need of help, one had but to say 'It's Korban—anything of mine that might have been of use to you . . .' and one would be in the impossibility of helping them. Strictly, the sentence should continue in verse 12: 'is no more at your service, for it is promised to God': but our Lord breaks off in disgust—'(the result is that) you no more allow him to do anything for his parents, cancelling out God's word by means of the tradition that *you* have handed down'. So our Lord does not answer the question about ablutions, but takes the offensive and attacks the value of the whole Pharisaic 'tradition' which had practically supplanted the Law.

68

The Law of God and Traditions of Men: (iii) 14–23

(Matt. 15: 10–20)

14. And calling again the multitude unto him, he said to them: Hear ye me all and understand.

15. There is nothing from without a man that entering into him can defile him. But the things which come from a man, those are they that defile a man.

16. If any man have ears to hear, let him hear.

17. And when he was come into the house from the multitude, his disciples asked him the parable.

18. And he saith to them: So are you also without knowledge? Understand you not that every thing from without entering into a man cannot defile him:

19. Because it entereth not into his heart but goeth into his belly and goeth out into the privy, purging all meats?

---

14. Our Lord offers to the crowds a principle which, being obscure, will need elucidation: it may be that the people had heard something of what Jesus said to the Pharisees, but naturally did not grasp the distinction between the 'material' and 'moral' orders which is familiar to us.

16. This verse acknowledges that there is a deeper contrast than that merely between what is taken into the mouth and what comes forth from it.

18. Our Lord suggests that by now the disciples ought to have grasped His meaning. He says with great realism that mere food, taken in through the mouth, passes (as we should say) through the digestive system, and then is got rid of, if it is 'waste product': 'Declaring that *all* foods are "pure"' is surely an exclamation of St Mark's echoing St Peter, who had not fully learnt that lesson till his vision reported in Acts 11. Material food does not reach what our Lord means by the 'heart', thought of as the home or source of moral virtues. He does not need to say that good thoughts, too, or impulses, proceed from within a man: He is occupied with what can

20. But he said that the things which come out from a man, they defile a man.

21. For from within, out of the heart of men, proceed evil thoughts, adulteries, fornications, murders,

22. Thefts, covetousness, wickedness, deceit, lasciviousness, an evil eye, blasphemy, pride, foolishness.

23. All these evil things come from within and defile man.

The Syro-Phoenician Woman: 24–30
(Matt. 15: 21–28)

24. And rising from thence he went into the coasts of Tyre and Sidon: and entering into a house, he would that no man should know it. And he could not be hid.

25. For a woman as soon as she heard of him, whose daughter had an unclean spirit, came in and fell down at his feet.

---

defile a man spiritually: hence the terrible list that follows—'wickedness' means malicious thoughts or acts; 'lasciviousness' (ἀσέλγεια) must mean a general looseness of life: 'evil eye', 'envy': 'blasphemy', all ill-speaking: ἀφροσύνη cannot mean merely 'foolishness'. It would not be an anti-climax if our Lord meant by it that *kind* of moral insensitiveness which means that a man has ended by killing, or at least paralysing, his conscience and is practically unaware of the difference between right and wrong, or has quite ceased to care about it. So St Paul (Rom. 1: 29–31) ends his list of pagan vices by four *negative* words: men without sympathy, without fidelity, without affection, without mercy (ἀσύνετοι, ἀσύνθετοι, ἄστοργοι, ἀνελεήμονες).

24. Presumably, leaving the neighbourhood of Capharnaum, He went north-west into the pagan territory (τὰ ὅρια), of Tyre; in 31 a distinction is made between the districts of Tyre and Sidon: the latter should perhaps be omitted here. The point is, that He withdrew from the jurisdiction of Herod.

25, 26. The woman was a pagan, a Phoenician from Syria

26. For the woman was a Gentile, a Syrophoenician born. And she besought him that he would cast forth the devil out of her daughter.
27. Who said to her: Suffer first the children to be filled: for it is not good
to take the bread of the children and cast it to the dogs.
28. But she answered and said to him: Yea, Lord; for the whelps also eat
under the table of the crumbs of the children.
29. And he said to her: For this saying, go thy way. The devil is gone out
of thy daughter.

(as contrasted with e.g. an Afro-Phoenician). 'Her little
daughter', θυγάτριον.
27. This verse is often made to sound too harsh, and the next, too
'pathetic'. 'Bread' (like 'meat') means 'food'. 'Cast'
(βαλεῖν) has a flavour of contempt about it: it simply means
'give'. 'Dogs', in the mouth of a Jew, can imply disgust—
dogs were scavengers (cf. Ps. 58: 7, 15; and Luke 16: 21,
where the beggar is so weak that he cannot even prevent the
dogs from licking his sores). But κύναρια is used in both
verses: there is no contrast between the grown dogs and poor
little puppies: κυνάρια μελιταῖα, in Malta, were actually
pet-dogs. (Jews had no current metaphor equating Gentiles
with 'dogs', though later, Mohammedans would speak of a
'dog of an unbeliever', and even we use the slang expression
'dirty dog'.) The only point is that the Faith must be offered
first to the Jew, and then, if rejected, to the Gentiles, as St
Paul himself was always to do. The woman says that she,
though a Gentile, must have her share—it would probably
be too elaborate to make her imply that the Gentiles ought
not to have to *wait*; since fragments of food were often
dropped or thrown on to the floor during a meal, the dogs
could eat at the same time as the family. Our Lord more than
once seems to begin with a refusal and then yields to faith and
trust (cf. the Miracle of Cana). St Mark is less severe than St
Matthew, and more vivid. He shows how pleased our Lord
was with the woman's humble, yet quick, reply, and, in a

30. And when she was come into her house, she found the girl lying upon the bed and that the devil was gone out.

A Deaf and Dumb Man Cured: 31–37
(Only in Mark)

31. And again going out of the coasts of Tyre, he came by Sidon to the sea of Galilee, through the midst of the coasts of Decapolis.
32. And they bring to him one deaf and dumb: and they besought him that he would lay his hand upon him.
33. And taking him from the multitude apart, he put his fingers into his ears: and spitting, he touched his tongue.
34. And looking up to heaven, he groaned and said to him: Ephpheta, which is, Be thou opened.
35. And immediately his ears were opened and the string of his tongue was loosed and he spoke right.

---

word or two, tells how the child was lying exhausted, but free, upon her bed.

31. We cannot tell exactly what route our Lord took, or why. Sidon is about a day's march north of Tyre: He then turned east to the Decapolis (see 5: 20: 'coasts' is Elizabethan English for 'region', without reference to the sea, cf. 24) which was still outside Herod's territory though 'towards' the Lake.

32. They brought to Him a deaf man who was μογιλάλος, i.e. not dumb, nor merely a stammerer, but who spoke with 'difficulty'; a serious impediment to speech. Why did He take him 'aside'? Perhaps because in a mainly pagan region He did not want His miracles to be misinterpreted as magical, as they would certainly be by men who could not connect them with His Messianic claims. St Matthew 15: 30, summarizes many miracles worked about this time, but not in this place.

33–35. This account seems exceptional, yet not altogether so. Sometimes our Lord worked His cures without any bodily intervention (e.g. that of the Syrophoenician's daughter just related); or again, by some simple form of help (e.g. lifting

36. And he charged them that they should tell no man. But the more he charged them, so much the more a great deal did they publish it.

37. And so much the more did they wonder, saying: He hath done all things well. He hath made both the deaf to hear and the dumb to speak.

Simon's mother-in-law; 1: 31), or, here, by a more elaborate, almost ritual, method. The man could not hear: our Lord puts His fingers into his ears—his ears are 'opened' to hear: He touches the man's tongue with His saliva, and the 'bond' of his tongue was loosed and he spoke *properly*. Putting His fingers into a deaf man's ears, touching his tongue with 'loosening' saliva, would not enable him to resolve to hear or speak, if he really could not: but a bodily act may encourage a man to accept a spiritual activity. We see that our Lord never despised material things. In Baptism, He uses water: in Confirmation, Ordination, the 'Last Anointing', He uses oil: in the Holy Eucharist, He uses bread and wine. Our Lord never scorns anything that we are, or are accustomed to. The use of saliva in Baptism is no longer obligatory, and no doubt will gradually be omitted. 'Symbols' are not always meaningful. So what our Lord *did* need not always be physically repeated save when He explicitly ordered it, e.g. the use of water in baptism; bread and wine in the Eucharist. Christ's religion will always be 'sacramental', i.e. will respect *all that is in us*: we are 'body' as truly as we are 'soul'. Even when in heaven, we shall not be angels!

CHAPTER EIGHT

The Second Feeding of the Multitude: 1–10

(Matt. 15: 32–39)

1. In those days again, when there was a great multitude and they had nothing to eat; calling his disciples together, he saith to them:
2. I have compassion on the multitude, for behold they have now been with me three days and have nothing to eat.
3. And if I shall send them away fasting to their home, they will faint in the way: for some of them came from afar off.
4. And his disciples answered him: From whence can any one fill them here with bread in the wilderness?

---

1. The time and place are left vague; but our Lord must have been still in the Decapolis and preaching, for He would not have allowed crowds to collect, and remain, simply to show them miracles (see end of Chapter 7).

2, 3. 'Three days' ($ἤδη$ $ἡμέραι$ $τρεῖς$) is nominative: a sort of parenthetical exclamation: '—three whole days!—' This unusual construction is also in Matthew (15: 32); and $νήστεις$, 'fasting', is to be found, in the Scriptures, only in Matthew and Mark—enough to show either that they used an identical written source, or, that one of them copied the other (see p. x). Read 'and', not 'for' (some of them are from far off).

4. 'Whence' ($πόθεν$) simply means 'How?' It is incredible that the disciples should have forgotten the previous miracle (even if they had not seen the point of it): but in the former case, their question (6: 37) was almost ironic: here it seems almost a shy suggestion that He should repeat that miracle. St Mark is true to his 'realism': he cannot say they lay down on the

74

5. And he asked them: How many loaves have ye? Who said: Seven.
6. And taking the seven loaves, giving thanks, he broke and gave to his disciples for to set before them. And they set them before the people.
7. And they had a few little fishes: and he blessed them and commanded them to be set before them.
8. And they did eat and were filled: and they took up that which was left of the fragments, seven baskets.
9. And they that had eaten were about four thousand. And he sent them away.
10. And immediately going up into a ship with his disciples, he came into the parts of Dalmanutha.

A 'Sign from the Sky': 11–13
(Matt. 16: 1–4; Luke 11: 29–32)

11. And the Pharisees came forth and began to question with him, asking him a sign from heaven, tempting him.

'green grass': now all grass was withered. The Greek has: 'And he commanded the people to sit down on the ground. And taking . . .'.

8. A σφυρίς was much larger than a κόφινος: a sort of plaited crate, not a basket: St Paul (Acts 9: 25) was placed in one to be let down from a window. The fact that they had some fishes does not prove they were near the Lake: salted fish could be kept a long time.

10. St Mark's favourite εὐθύς does not mean more than 'then', 'afterwards'. Dalmanutha is not precisely known, but it is clearly on the west side of the Lake. St Matthew (15: 39) has 'Magedan' (some MSS. have 'Magdala', but when the story of Mary of Magdala became known, this is an 'easier' emendation and so, less trustworthy). Magedan *may* be the modern El Mejdel, which was presumably the homeland of Mary Magdalene: but since the place is left vague—'into the region of'—St Peter may well have remembered it in terms of one township and St Matthew in terms of a neighbouring one.

11. The Pharisees 'come forth' from the town to the place where Jesus had disembarked: they began to 'question' Him;

12. And sighing deeply in spirit, he saith: Why doth this generation seek a sign? Amen, I say to you, a sign shall not be given to this generation.

13. And leaving them, he went up again into the ship and passed to the other side of the water.

συνζητεῖν means that they had joined in a discussion, the upshot being a demand for a 'sign from the sky', like the fire brought down by Elias (1 Kings 18: 38; 2 Kings 1: 10): this would test Him! If He failed, He was no Messias! But it is clear that our Lord, though He worked many miracles of mercy, never would provide any simply for His own glorification.

12. 'Sighing deeply in spirit', that is, He recognized that they were asking for a miracle insincerely—they felt sure He would be unable to provide what they asked; and even had He provided the *sort* of sign they asked, they would have found a way of rejecting it: He was not the kind of Messias they wanted! In Matt. 12: 38 and 16: 4, and Luke 9: 29, a 'sign' is asked for and our Lord refuses any other than that of the prophet Jonas, whose history prefigured his own death and resurrection. Why does St Mark omit this striking sentence? No doubt a 'sign' was often asked for, and on some different occasion our Lord did allude to Jonas: but the incidents related in Matthew 12 and Mark 11 are not 'parallel' to that related by St Mark: Jonas may well have been alluded to *then*. When Matthew in Chapter 16 *is* parallel, it is quite possible that the allusion to Jonas was inserted by a copyist who had the other passages in mind: this is far more probable than that St Mark omitted so striking a sentence if it had formed part of the tradition of *this* episode. Anyhow 'Jonas' would have meant nothing to readers mainly Roman. 'A sign shall not be given.' The Greek εἰ δοθήσεται is a literal translation of a Hebrew way of speaking: e.g. 'If I am telling a lie . . . (may God strike me dead)'. The meaning would be: 'I am *not* telling a lie', though the second half of the phrase would not be spoken. So here: 'If a sign shall be given . . .' means: 'A sign shall certainly *not* be given'.

The Leaven of the Pharisees: 14–21
(Matt. 16: 5–12; cf. Luke 12: 1)

14. And they forgot to take bread: and they had but one loaf with them in the ship.

15. And he charged them, saying: Take heed and beware of the leaven of the Pharisees and of the leaven of Herod.

16. And they reasoned among themselves, saying: Because we have no bread.

17. Which Jesus knowing, saith to them: Why do you reason, because you have no bread? Do you not yet know nor understand? Have you still your heart blinded?

18. Having eyes, see you not? And having ears, hear you not? Neither do you remember?

14, 15. Perhaps the sequence of thoughts is as follows. Our Lord 'began to urge on them—Be on the alert! be on your guard against the leaven of the Pharisees and Herodians!' Then they saw they had brought no bread.

16. Thereupon 'They began to argue *at* one another, about not having any bread'. They failed even to attend to our Lord's words and any spiritual meaning they might contain. Our Lord was warning them against two sorts of 'infection', so to say; 'leaven' might be taken in a favourable sense, as in Matt. 13: 33; Luke 13: 21; or again in the opposite sense, as here, and e.g. 1 Cor. 5: 6; Gal. 5: 9—the point being the same, i.e. something very small (like a pinch of leaven) can permeate and alter something much larger than itself (like a lump of dough). The behaviour of the Pharisees was too rigid (at least exteriorly), and that of the Herodian court too lax. Let them beware of both extremes!

17–21. The severity of our Lord's rebuke may surprise us; but it was spoken entirely in Old Testament phraseology (e.g. Jer. 5: 21; Ezech. 12: 2). He was 'hurt' because the disciples, instead of listening to what He was saying, started at once to argue about the bread—presumably 'Whose fault was it that

77

19. When I broke the five loaves among five thousand, how many baskets full of fragments took you up? They say to him: Twelve.
20. When also the seven loaves among four thousand, how many baskets of fragments took you up? And they said to him Seven.
21. And he said to them: How do you not yet understand?

A Blind Man Cured: 22–26

(Only in Mark)

22. And they came to Bethsaida: and they bring to him a blind man. And they besought him that he would touch him.
23. And taking the blind man by the hand, he led him out of the town. And spitting upon his eyes, laying his hands on him, he asked him if he saw any thing.
24. And looking up, he said: I see men, as it were trees, walking.
25. After that again he laid his hands upon his eyes: and he began to see and was restored, so that he saw all things clearly.
26. And he sent him into his house, saying: Go into thy house, and if thou enter into the town, tell nobody.

---

they had none?'; and because, in any case, if need be, could He not work a miracle? not that counting on a miracle would have excused them for not taking trouble to make due preparations!

22. If verse 10 places Dalmanutha on the west coast, verse 13 shows that they, having crossed the lake, found Bethsaida on the east (cf. 6: 45). But since it is agreed that St Mark did not write his records in any strict 'order', we cannot assume that these incidents followed one another chronologically: the incident related in verses 13–17 may have been placed where it is because the mention of the Pharisees just before brought it to his mind; so we cannot tell why they reached Bethsaida, nor whence, nor on which side of the lake it was.

22–26. This miracle is related by St Mark only: it has special, though not unique, details. Our Lord leads the blind man by the hand, out of the town (so had He helped Simon's mother-in-law to rise: 1: 31): some of His miracles were not for

78

The 'Confession' of St Peter: 27–30

(Matt. 16: 13–20; Luke 9: 18–21)

27. And Jesus went out, and his disciples, into the towns of Cæsarea Philippi. And in the way, he asked his disciples, saying to them: Whom do men say that I am?

---

publication, and none were for 'ostentation' only: others were meant to 'prove a point' (3: 5). Here He cures the man out of kindness, and privately, sends him home and tells him not so much as to return into the 'village', as we might say, into the old Bethsaida which had become a sort of 'suburb' of the new expanding town. (It was an *order*: not 'if thou enter', as above.) What is unparalleled is the gradual character of the cure. Our Lord establishes confidence by leading the man by personal contact into a private place. He then uses saliva which was considered to have a special value in curing eyes, but *also* lays His hands on him. He asks: 'Do you see anything?' He says: 'I see men—like trees, only walking!' This (to my mind) neither proves nor disproves that he was not blind from birth. A birth-blind man can perfectly well learn by touch what a tree is; but if he sees that what might be a tree, but is *moving*, knowing that men move, he would easily cry out: 'That can't be a tree, but a man!' However, when our Lord again touched his eyes, he saw τηλαυγῶς, 'distinctly', and at a distance. This suggests the man had been extremely short-sighted, rather like the man who was μογιλάλος, who spoke, but spoke with difficulty (7: 31 ff.). It is interesting that only St Mark relates these miracles where saliva, etc., are used. St Mark's words are carefully chosen: (24) ἀναβλέπειν: to lift one's eyes to look: (25) διαβλέπειν: saw through the dimness that still had remained; then, ἀπεκατέστη, he was perfectly cured, and ἐνέβλεπεν (imperfect, in contrast with the two previous aorists): 'he was seeing everything distinctly'.

27. The 'towns' mean the various small places belonging to the head-town, Cæsarea Philippi. Augustus gave this territory to

28. Who answered him, saying: John the Baptist; but some Elias, and others as one of the prophets.

29. Then he saith to them: But whom do you say that I am? Peter answering said to him: Thou art the Christ.

30. And he strictly charged them that they should not tell any man of him.

Our Lord's Passion Prophesied: 31–33
(Matt. 16: 21–23; Luke 9: 22)

31. And he began to teach them that the Son of man must suffer many things and be rejected by the ancients and by the high priests and the scribes: and be killed and after three days rise again.

Herod the Great, who built a temple in honour of the Emperor close to the grotto whence a main source of the Jordan gushes. This grotto was treated as a shrine of the god Pan (who probably replaced an earlier Baal) and the neighbouring town, built by the tetrarch Philip, was called Cæsarea Philippi in his own and the Emperor's honour (in distinction from Cæsarea on the sea side); but the pagan name has survived in the form Banias.

28. With this verse cf. 6: 14, 15. On the way, our Lord asked who people were saying that He was. 'John the Baptist come to life again—or Elias—or that you are "a" prophet'. It is not strange that no one had suggested 'the Messias', because not even Elias was expected to come, like the Messias, in 'glory'. But it *is*, humanly speaking, amazing that Peter, in reply to 'But who do *you* (emphatic) say that I am?' so firmly answered: 'Thou art the *Christ*!' St Matthew (16: 17 ff.), adds much more to the glory, we may say, of St Peter and the future constitution of the Church: but the sole point here is, the recognition of the Messias in the humble person of Jesus: St Peter, in these few words, had said everything. It is possible that humility kept him back from repeating the tremendous words that our Lord addressed to him personally; or, even, that it may have been thought unwise to give 'publicity' to

80

32. And he spoke the word openly. And Peter taking him, began to rebuke him.

33. Who turning about and seeing his disciples, threatened Peter, saying: Go behind me, Satan, because thou savourest not the things that are of God but that are of men.

---

what might seem even remotely the setting up of a rival to the Roman Empire. Our Lord Himself (30) insisted that, for the time, the disciples should keep their conviction to themselves.

31. Our Lord begins now to concentrate on the fact that the Messias (whom they have acknowledged Him to be) must be *rejected* by His own people and their leaders. The 'ancients', 'elders', were probably the more important of the lay upper classes—seniority does not here imply old age: there was strictly only one high priest who held his office for life: but here 'high priests' probably means the more important members of priestly families. 'After three days' means a day and part of the days coming before and after it. This expression was less clear than 'on the third day' which became normal (e.g. Matt. 16: 21; Luke 9: 22; Acts 10: 40; 1 Cor. 15: 4, and often).

32. He spoke 'explicitly': there was no chance of misunderstanding him. Peter was 'shocked': 'taking him', προσλαβόμενος, means 'taking him to himself' for encouragement, rather than 'taking him to one side': (cf. Rom. 14: 1, 3; 15: 7, etc.). He began to 'reproach' him: the word is the same as that used in v. 33; there is no reason for translating it 'rebuke' in the former verse, and 'threaten' in the latter.

33. We could translate Ὕπαγε ὀπίσω μου: 'Back, and follow me!' but the use of the word 'Satan', i.e. 'adversary', necessitates the translation: 'Away! behind with you!'— 'Savourest' (οὐ φρονεῖς), 'You do not think as God thinks, but human thoughts!' 'Relish' is a translation of the Vulgate *sapis*, which does not translate the Greek. If our Lord's 'reproach' seems almost too vehement, we remember that

H

The Following of Christ: 34–39

(Matt. 16: 24–28; Luke 9: 23–27)

34. And calling the multitude together with his disciples, he said to them: If any man will follow me, let him deny himself and take up his cross and follow me.

35. For whosoever will save his life shall lose it: and whosoever shall lose his life for my sake and the gospel shall save it.

36. For what shall it profit a man, if he gain the whole world and suffer the loss of his soul?

His human nature shrank terribly from the Passion He foresaw: the 'Agony' in Gethsemani was but an intensified form of what He endured throughout His life at the prospect of His rejection, cruel sufferings, and death.

34. Our Lord now definitely extends His doctrine of self-sacrifice to the general listeners, but in less detail than He had to the disciples. Still, (1) He places Himself at the centre—'if any man will follow *me*'—and (2) proceeds to say that this will mean the total denial, renunciation of self, even should this involve actual death by crucifixion. Nor was there a contradiction between thus putting Himself at the 'centre' and then demanding self-abdication from all others, because He Himself was going to carry a cross and to die upon it. Though our Lord's listeners could hardly have supposed that He was definitely foreshadowing their crucifixion, still less, that He was speaking 'mystically', as St Paul did (Gal. 2: 19: 'I am co-crucified with Christ'), yet we recall that crucifixion was quite a common punishment, especially for anything that even looked like rebellion.

35, 36. The word ψυχή can mean either 'life', i.e. physical existence, or 'soul', i.e. the spiritual part of man which survives hereafter. What our Lord says, first, is that those who propose to 'follow' Him must expect, even on earth, to lead a life of self-renunciation, even up to dying a cruel death—and the history of the Martyrs showed that this was

37. Or what shall a man give in exchange for his soul?

38. For he that shall be ashamed of me and of my words, in this adulterous and sinful generation: the Son of man also will be ashamed of him, when he shall come in the glory of his Father with the holy angels.

39. And he said to them: Amen I say to you that there are some of them that stand here who shall not taste death till they see the kingdom of God coming in power.

---

true: and secondly, that no amount of winning the material goods obtainable in this world can 'ransom' the 'forfeiting' of His everlasting and truest life in the next.

38. This marvellous verse sets in contrast two whole worlds—the world which is 'sinful' and apostate from God (as, in a special way, the Jewish contemporary world was, which regarded itself as 'wedded' to God) and the world of God, of His unique Son who is also the Son of Man, and of all the 'holy angels' (that is, all spirits who are obedient to Him and form His 'escort'). The word for 'to be ashamed of', ἐπαισχύνεσθαι, to blush at, in someone's presence, is used here alone in the Gospel (save St Luke, who is parallel to this passage), though seven times in St Paul, and means that those who (knowingly) think themselves above Christ and His doctrine, and therefore God and all who in heaven or on earth are 'one' with Him, will be held as shameful by God Himself.

39. This verse creates a difficulty both as to what it means in itself, and how it is connected with what precedes. St Mark's words 'and He said to them' suggest a separate statement. When was it said? And was this said to everyone, or to the disciples only? If to everyone, was it meant to remain enigmatic? It certainly would have done so! 'Some of those standing here' cannot refer to *all* who were present, and indeed suggests a few, rather than many. 'Shall not taste of death' simply means 'shall not die', and this seems to exclude identifying the Coming of the Kingdom with the Transfiguration, for that took place in about a week, and our Lord

could hardly have said: 'Some of you will be alive in a week's time.' Nor can our Lord have referred to the End of the World, which was to be His Coming in *glory*, which is different from 'with power', and St Paul (e.g. Rom. 1: 4; 15: 19; 1 Cor. 4: 20) connects our Lord's 'power' with His resurrection, with the Holy Spirit, and their manifestation in the marvellous preaching of the Gospel with its attendant miracles. Luke 9: 27, says simply 'till they see the kingdom of God': Matt. 16: 28, 'till they see the Son of Man coming in His Kingdom'. It seems then impossible to be sure what was the original form of this sentence: the reason for its being placed where it is may be 'association of ideas' due to the word 'coming' found here and in the previous verse: possibly what our Lord foretold was that some few of those there present would see and *understand* the Coming of the Son of Man 'in power', i.e. in the miraculous development of His Church after Pentecost—for the sorrowful fact remains that most who did 'see' it with their eyes remained spiritually blinded to what it signified.[1]

---

[1] It is true that a certain number of the Fathers (including St John Chrysostom) consider this passage to allude to the Transfiguration, and sometimes the 'saying' is attached to what follows, not, as here, to what precedes. But even allowing for the highly-coloured oriental way of speaking, we think the arguments adduced above hold good.

CHAPTER NINE

The Transfiguration: 1-8
(Matt. 17: 1-8; Luke 9: 28-36. Cf. 2 Peter 1: 16 ff.)

1. And after six days, Jesus taketh with him Peter and James and John, and leadeth them up into an high mountain apart by themselves, and was transfigured before them.
2. And his garments became shining and exceeding white as snow, so as no fuller upon earth can make white.

---

1. 'Apart by themselves' (κατ' ἰδίαν μόνους) (cf. 4: 34; 6: 31, 32, etc.): this mountain may have been Tabor, some miles south-east of Nazareth and standing apart—only, the words quoted above do not refer to the mountain but to the solitude in which Jesus placed the apostles. Others think it was Hermon, not far from Caesarea Philippi whence our Lord had come. St Jerome and St Cyril of Jerusalem decide for Tabor. But the earlier tradition is quite confused. Strictly speaking, *transfigurari* would represent the Greek μετασχηματίζεσθαι. The Greek word μεταμόρφουσθαι implies an interior change: St Paul uses both words (2 Cor. 3: 18; Phil. 3: 21): 'shining' (στίλβοντα), occurs only here in the New Testament: the reference to the 'fuller' or laundry-man is so naïve as to be thoroughly Marcan.
2. 'As snow' is probably introduced into the original by a writer who remembered Daniel 7: 9. St Mark was not an expert in shades of meaning; but he surely intends to imply that the change in our Lord's appearance was not merely external: the true glory that was His by nature began to shine through His humanity; though even so, it was not the glory of God

85

3. And there appeared to them Elias with Moses: and they were talking with Jesus.

4. And Peter answering, said to Jesus: Rabbi, it is good for us to be here. And let us make three tabernacles, one for thee, and one for Moses, and one for Elias.

5. For he knew not what he said: for they were struck with fear.

6. And there was a cloud over-shadowing them. And a voice came out of the cloud, saying: This is my most beloved Son. Hear ye him.

7. And immediately looking about, they saw no man any more, but Jesus only with them.

---

that no mortal eye can endure (He 'dwells in light inaccessible': 1 Tim. 6: 16): but even though symbolical, our Lord's glory was no mere reflected light, such as shone upon the face of Moses after his colloquy with God (Ex. 34: 29).

3. Elias came *with* Moses (who retains thus the senior rank): they stand for the Law and the Prophets and speak harmoniously with Jesus: there is no harsh break with the past. St Mark does not say, as St Luke does (11: 31), that they were speaking of His imminent 'departure'.

4, 5. 'Answering' is an Aramaism, as so often, for no one had spoken to him: it simply means 'spoke, and said . . .' Most probably Peter means: 'It is fortunate that we three disciples are here, so as to build three huts, etc.': even if the more pious meaning be accepted—'It is good for us to be here'— he would still imply that he imagined that our Lord and Moses and Elias meant to stay there, in fact, that the glorious Messianic reign had begun. Such brushwood shelters were easily built, and in fact the Jews made and lived in them during the Feast of Tabernacles, or Tents. St Mark 'apologizes' for him—he did not realize what he was saying, or, know what to say, for they were terrified out of their wits. This was not, however, mere *fright*; they were overwhelmed with a religious awe.

6. The Cloud was the exterior manifestation of the divine presence (Ex. 16: 10; 19: 9, 16; 33: 9): it overshadowed the

8. And as they came down from the mountain, he charged them not to tell any man what things they had seen, till the Son of man shall be risen again from the dead.

The Passion again Predicted: 9–12
(Matt. 17: 9–13; cf. Luke 9: 36b)

9. And they kept the word to themselves; questioning together what that should mean, when he shall be risen from the dead.

10. And they asked him saying: Why then do the Pharisees and scribes say that Elias must come first?

Tabernacle (Ex. 11: 29): 'overshadow' must not suggest darkness: the Holy Ghost, and the 'Power of the Most High' overshadowed Mary (Luke 1: 35). The Voice proclaims the relation of Jesus with His Father—it repeats and reinforces the Proclamation at the Baptism: this scene does indeed inaugurate the second part of our Lord's Ministry, and was the more needed since from now on he moves steadily towards Calvary.

7. 'Immediately' (ἐξάπινα) occurs only here in the New Testament. The vision was swiftly over—they looked round, and found no one with them, save Jesus only.

8. Either hearers would believe too readily if they were told of this event, and would wish to acclaim the Messias-King; or they might be unable to assimilate any of the story and come to be in bad faith, refusing to believe even what they could and should have believed, the three witnesses being who they were. After the Resurrection, it would be easier to accept the earlier marvels, especially as these had included the foretelling of the Passion.

9. They 'kept fast to what He had said'; i.e. did as He had told them, and held their tongue save among themselves: they did, however, wonder what He could mean by 'rising from the dead', since He had already appeared in glory.

10. Still, they approach the topic indirectly. 'Why do the Scribes (omit 'the Pharisees') say that Elias must come first?' They

11. Who answering, said to them: Elias, when he shall come first, shall restore all things; and as it is written of the Son of man that he must suffer many things and be despised.

12. But I say to you that Elias also is come (and they have done to him whatsoever they would), as it is written of him.

The Epileptic Boy: 13–28
(Matt. 17: 14–20; Luke 9: 37–43)

13. And coming to his disciples he saw a great multitude about them and the scribes disputing with them.

14. And presently all the people, seeing Jesus, were astonished and struck with fear; and running to him, they saluted him.

---

remembered Mal. 4: 5: 'Behold, I will send you Elias the prophet, before the coming of the great and dreadful day of the Lord.' As it was, in the vision Elias did *not* come first, and departed without playing his due role of preparation. Further, if he is still to come, and achieve a general conversion, how shall the Messias be rejected?

11. The meaning is: 'Elias arrives first, and restores all to order—(if that is so) how then is it written that the Son of Man must suffer much and be set at naught?' The answer is, that the role of Elias has been misinterpreted.

12. Elias *has* come, in the person of the Baptist, and both the original Elias and John of whom he was the type suffered for righteousness' sake at the hands of a weak king and a wicked woman (see 3 Kings 17–19): 'they worked their will upon him': if, then, John was killed, what reason is there against the Messias being slain? Since our Lord interprets the whole prophecy symbolically, there is no need for us to expect a literal physical reappearance of Elias at the 'last day'.

13. What were they 'discussing'? Possibly why the disciples could not cure the boy. But the Scribes do not reappear and the discussion can be disregarded.

14. 'Struck with fear' (ἐκθαμβεῖσθαι only here and Mark 14: 33 and 16: 6, 7, where it denotes a stupefying fear): why

88

15. And he asked them: What do you question about among you?
16. And one of the multitude, answering, said: Master, I have brought my son to thee, having a dumb spirit.
17. Who, wheresoever he taketh him, dasheth him: and he foameth and gnasheth with the teeth and pineth away. And I spoke to thy disciples to cast him out: and they could not.
18. Who answering them, said: O incredulous generation, how long shall I be with you? How long shall I suffer you? Bring him unto me.
19. And they brought him. And when he had seen him, immediately the spirit troubled him: and being thrown down upon the ground, he rolled about foaming.
20. And he asked his father: How long time is it since this hath happened unto him? But he said: From his infancy.
21. And oftentimes hath he cast him into the fire and into waters to destroy him. But if thou canst do any thing, help us, having compassion on us.
22. And Jesus saith to him: If thou canst believe, all things are possible to him that believeth.

---

were they, first, awestruck, and then, hastening to meet him? Perhaps no more is meant than that they had not at all expected to see our Lord, but, overcoming their first shock of surprise, they ran to Him to ask His help.
16. The demon was 'dumb' because it refused to speak when adjured to do so. 'Lays hold of him' ($\kappa\alpha\tau\alpha\lambda\acute{\alpha}\beta\eta$): $\acute{\rho}\acute{\eta}\sigma\sigma\epsilon\iota$: 'throws him down': $\xi\eta\rho\alpha\acute{\iota}\nu\epsilon\tau\alpha\iota$: 'becomes rigid', literally, 'dry'. All these are symptoms of epilepsy.
18. 'Men of little faith!' The father had *some* faith, for he brought the boy to our Lord; so had the disciples, for they tried to exorcize the spirit: but by now they should have had more. Our Lord speaks as though His patience were exhausted; but no: 'Bring him to me!'
21. 'If thou canst . . .' Though disheartened by the failure of the apostles, He continued to hope against hope.
22. Our Lord takes up the man's words: 'Your "if thou canst"! All things are possible to one who believes!' The Vulgate

23. And immediately the father of the boy crying out, with tears said: I do believe, Lord. Help my unbelief.

24. And when Jesus saw the multitude running together, he threatened the unclean spirit, saying to him: Deaf and dumb spirit, I command thee, go out of him and enter not any more into him.

25. And crying out and greatly tearing him, he went out of him. And he became as dead, so that many said: He is dead.

26. But Jesus taking him by the hand, lifted him up. And he arose.

27. And when he was come into the house, his disciples secretly asked him: Why could not we cast him out?

28. And he said to them: This kind can go out by nothing, but by prayer and fasting.

(and various MSS.) fail to realize that our Lord is quoting the man's words, and inserts 'believe'—'if thou canst believe, all things, etc.'. The man, with a loud cry (and many MSS. and the Vulgate add, 'and tears') exclaimed: 'I believe! help my unbelief!', that is, the man knew he believed—up to a point; might he be helped in so far as his faith was inadequate?

24. Either a new crowd kept running up, or our Lord had taken the man aside, but now was pursued by the excited throng. Our Lord 'rebukes' the spirit, with absolute authority, and forbids its return.

25. The participles 'crying out' (κράξας) and 'tearing' (σπαράξας) are in the masculine, corrected by some to suit the neuter 'pneuma' (πνεῦμα). As before (20), a spirit 'possessing' a man becomes in some sort one with him. Despite this last display of diabolic power, and the convulsions and then collapse of the boy, our Lord is seen the stronger.

27, 28. The disciples cannot understand how they could not do what they had been promised they should do (6: 7) and had succeeded in doing: our Lord seems to say that evil spirits—perhaps some specially strong spirits—cannot be cast out without prayer (many MSS. add 'and fasting'): presumably the disciples had relied too much on their own powers.

A Third Prediction of the Passion: 29–31

(Matt. 17: 22, 23; Luke 9: 43–45)

29. And departing from thence, they passed through Galilee: and he would not that any man should know it.

30. And he taught his disciples and said to them: The Son of man shall be betrayed into the hands of men, and they shall kill him; and after that he is killed, he shall rise again the third day.

31. But they understood not the word: and they were afraid to ask him.

---

29. 'Thence.' This sounds as if the mountain had not been Tabor, for this was well in the middle of Galilee: but if it had been e.g. Hermon, up near Cæsarea Philippi, a journey to Jerusalem by way of Capharnaum could easily have been described as 'passing through Galilee'. Why this 'incognito'? Possibly because He wanted to be free to instruct the apostles, but perhaps because other groups of pilgrims would have been going to Jerusalem, and might have become enthusiastic about His appearance, and have accompanied Him to the Holy City as a popular hero, if not the Messias Himself. How-

30. ever, St Mark himself writes: '*For* he was teaching . . .': the Vulgate changes this to *autem*, and the Douay has simply 'and'. Moreover, St Mark writes 'is being betrayed' ($\pi\alpha\rho\alpha\delta\iota\delta\sigma\tau\alpha\iota$), for which St Matthew and St Luke put the future, 'shall be handed over', referring thus to the betrayal yet to come: we cannot suppose that Judas was already negotiating the betrayal, so St Mark must mean that the Son of Man was in fact on the way, even now, to being handed over to men.

31. The disciples had the fixed idea that the Messias could not be killed; therefore they were at a loss as to what our Lord could *mean* by saying that He would be: they were shy of asking Him what He did not choose to explain to them, or possibly had a latent fear that He really meant what He said—a possibility to which they would not consciously attend.

We now enter upon a series of 'instructions' which are not essentially interconnected, but are linked together, apparently

Being like Children: 32–36

(Matt. 18: 1–5; Luke 9: 46–48)

32. And they came to Capharnaum. And when they were in the house, he asked them: What did you treat of in the way?

33. But they held their peace, for in the way they had disputed among themselves, which of them should be the greatest.

34. And sitting down, he called the twelve and saith to them: If any man desire to be first, he shall be the last of all and the minister of all.

35. And taking a child, he set him in the midst of them. Whom when he had embraced, he saith to them:

---

because some word or thought in a preceding section suggests the following to St Mark personally.

32. 'The' house: Peter's? or Levi's? He felt at home there. Evidently He had walked ahead; still, He knew what they had discussed without their telling Him, which they were no doubt ashamed to do.

34. He sat down, naturally; for they had been walking and were tired. 'He shall be . . .' practically, 'let him be, behave as. . . .' There would certainly be a 'hierarchy' in the Kingdom upon earth: but let not precedence be sought out of ambition!

35. Only St Mark says that our Lord embraced the child: but what was a child doing there, while our Lord was instructing the apostles? The comment on their behaviour was surely a private one?[1] It is possible that the incident occurred in a different setting, but is inserted here as aptly illustrating our Lord's theme of humility. Presumably the 'child' stands, first, literally for 'children', but further, for any weak or helpless people who are to be received in our Lord's name— i.e. for His sake. Others compare 'receive, etc.' with 6: 11, and 'in my name' as 'invested with my authority', and that the 'child' therefore represents the simple unlearned apostles.

[1] But what more likely, in Palestine, than that a small child wandered in—that the apostles started to turn it out, and that our Lord said 'Not at all! This is just what you've got to be like!'

36. Whosoever shall receive one such child as this in my name receiveth me. And whosoever shall receive me receiveth not me but him that sent me.

The Cup of Water: 37-41
(Luke 9: 49-50)

37. John answered him, saying: Master, we saw one casting out devils in thy name, who followeth not us: and we forbade him.

38. But Jesus said: Do not forbid him. For there is no man that doth a miracle in my name and can soon speak ill of me.

39. For he that is not against you is for you.

40. For whosoever shall give you to drink a cup of water in my name, because you belong to Christ: amen I say to you, he shall not lose his reward.

The scene is described differently by St Matthew, but the doctrine is the same.

36. 'Receiveth not me . . .': i.e. 'not merely me, but my Father who sent me'. They are inseparable.

37. 'Answering' is not in the best MSS. The link with what precedes is the use of our Lord's Name. 'Forbade'; but ἐκωλύομεν, is in the imperfect: 'we tried to forbid him': 'were forbidding him'.

39. Our Lord argues that if a man uses His name, he at least recognizes His authority. If he proceeded to speak ill of Jesus, he would be contradicting himself. We should read 'against, for, *us*': our Lord regards Himself and the apostles as forming a unit. But in Matthew 12: 30, and Luke 11: 23, cf. 9: 50, He says: 'He that is not with me, is against me; and he that gathereth not with me, scattereth.' The point is really the same: one cannot be neutral about our Lord. In Matthew and Luke 'not to be *with*' indicates hostility: in Mark, the use of His name indicates good will.[1]

---

[1] It is quite possible that our Lord spoke two sentences, seemingly contradictory but really complementary: or again that in a Gentile world the saying became softened down while in Matthew's Jewish world its rigour was retained. We still think that our Lord used both expressions, in different circumstances.

41. And whosoever shall scandalize one of these little ones that believe in me: it were better for him that a millstone were hanged about his neck and he were cast into the sea.

More about 'Scandal': 42–49

(Matt. 18: 6, 8, 9; and 5: 13; Luke 5: 29–30; 14: 34–35)

42. And if thy hand scandalize thee, cut it off: it is better for thee to enter into life, maimed, than having two hands to go into hell, into unquenchable fire:

---

40. John's interruption brings the talk back to what precedes (verse 38): '*for* if anyone gives you even a cup of water because you belong to Christ', he shall be rewarded. The expression is unparalleled in the Synoptists or Acts, where 'Christ' is never used without the article, though it occurs in St Paul (Rom. 7: 9; 1 Cor. 1: 12; 3: 23; 2 Cor. 10: 7). Though Peter had acknowledged His Messiahship, the title had not yet become current.

41. We have come right back to the starting point: 'scandalize' (σκάνδαλον: a stumbling-block): the verb means to put something in a man's way that may trip him up: as for one who puts temptation in another's way, especially a weaker or helpless person's—(μύλος ὀνικός) a mill-stone turned by a donkey, heavier therefore than a hand-turned mill-stone. The 'donkey-mill' was composed of a saucer-shaped stone with a hole in the middle. On this was placed another stone with a pivot passing through the hole. The grain would be poured into the 'nether mill-stone' and be crushed against the pivot as the upper mill-stone was turned. The perforated stone could be slung round a man's neck, and the Romans in fact used this at times as a form of capital punishment. If a Jew hired a house, he could put in a 'donkey-mill' but not a handmill, which made much more noise.

42–48. We may not only be a 'scandal' to others, but be attached to something which may make *us* stumble and fall: however close this object, or occupation, or person, may be, we must

43. Where their worm dieth not, and the fire is not extinguished.

44. And if thy foot scandalize thee, cut it off: it is better for thee to enter lame into life everlasting than having two feet to be cast into the hell of unquenchable fire:

45. Where their worm dieth not, and the fire is not extinguished.

46. And if thy eye scandalize thee, pluck it out: it is better for thee with one eye to enter into the kingdom of God than having two eyes to be cast into the hell of fire:

'detach' ourselves from it—an act of renunciation symbolized by the cutting off of hand or foot, or the plucking out of an eye. 'Life' is identified in verse 46 with the Kingdom of God (in 44, 'everlasting' seems to be an explanatory addition). The opposite to this is 'Gehenna'. A valley near Jerusalem was called Gei Hinnom, where children had been thrown into fire in honour of the god Moloch: trumpets and cymbals drowned their cries (4 Kings, 23: 10; Jer. 7: 31, 32): King Josias stopped this practice. Afterwards the valley was known as the place where criminals were executed; then, the wicked were to be punished there; finally, the name Gehenna was given to the place of their after-death punishment and is equivalent to 'hell'. 'Where their worm dieth not and the fire is not extinguished' should probably be read only in verse 47: it is a quotation from Is. 66: 24, and refers directly to the fate of the corpses of the Lord's enemies: but in a passage where so much is metaphorical, we cannot be sure when exactly the metaphor ends: the 'worm' is clearly metaphorical, and, so far as this passage goes we cannot assert that the 'fire' is *not*. For the nature of the pains of hell, and their enduring nature, we must ask the doctrine and tradition of the Church. In verse 48, the last part is lacking in the best MSS.: 'all must be salted with fire' recalls that 'salt' was regarded as a preservative: if, then, the wicked are salted with fire, this fire, acting like salt, does not consume, but preserves for ever: if *all* are to be 'salted with fire', we must assume that the renunciations spoken of above, fiery though they

47. Where their worm dieth not, and the fire is not extinguished.
48. For every one shall be salted with fire: and every victim shall be salted with salt.
49. Salt is good. But if the salt become unsavoury, wherewith will you season it? Have salt in you: and have peace among you.

---

seem, preserve the good from evil and purify them. 'For every victim shall be salted with salt' refers to the order in Lev. 2: 13: the 'salting' of a sacrifice would imply the *permanence* of the offerer's alliance with God. But quite possibly the words are a marginal note, trying to explain the obscure words that precede, though they contain no reference to *victims* as such.

49. We think that this is a detached logion, inserted here simply because the word 'salt' causes St Mark to remember it. Men need to have in them a 'preservative', a 'salt'; if this salt becomes 'de-salted' there is nothing that can make it salt again. In so far as the salt was connected with the idea of 'permanent alliance', we can see that 'keep peace among you' (εἰρηνεύατε) is not out of place here, especially if we recall that the whole instruction began because of the dispute among the apostles as to who should be the greatest among them.

CHAPTER TEN

Marriage: 1–12

(Matt. 19: 3–9; cf. Matthew 5: 31, 32; Luke 16: 18)

1. And rising up from thence, he cometh into the coasts of Judea beyond the Jordan: and the multitude flocked to him again. And as he was accustomed, he taught them again.
2. And the Pharisees coming to him asked him, tempting him: Is it lawful for a man to put away his wife?
3. But he answering, saith to them: What did Moses command you?
4. Who said: Moses permitted to write a bill of divorce and to put her away.

---

1. Our Lord therefore leaves Galilee for Judea and the region of trans-Jordan: 'and' must be added, for Judea had no territory beyond the Jordan. This took place probably in September in the year before the Passion; St Matthew and St Mark record only what occurred during the last two months of this period: St Luke (10: 51 to 19: 22) and St John (7: 10 to 11: 56) are much fuller.
2. The Pharisees 'test' Him, to see whether He would say anything against the authority of Moses.
3. Our Lord asks what Moses had 'commanded'. They knew he had commanded nothing, but *allowed* a 'writ of repudiation' to be given to his wife by a man determined to be rid of her: then, if she married again, her new husband could not create, or fear, difficulties. The school of the Rabbi Shammai held that this writ of repudiation could be given only for grave reasons—presumably infidelity: that of Hillel permitted it for the most frivolous reasons, e.g. if a wife spoilt the meals she cooked.

I

SAINT MARK

5. To whom Jesus answering, said: Because of the hardness of your heart, he wrote you that precept.
6. But from the beginning of the creation, God made them male and female.
7. For this cause, a man shall leave his father and mother and shall cleave to his wife.
8. And they two shall be in one flesh. Therefore now they are not two, but one flesh.
9. What therefore God hath joined together, let not man put asunder.
10. And in the house again his disciples asked him concerning the same thing.
11. And he saith to them: Whosoever shall put away his wife and marry another committeth adultery against her.

---

5. 'Hardness of heart'—nothing would have persuaded the Hebrews *not* to get rid of their wives when they wanted to: Moses could not force them to fidelity, and permitted a compromise.
6. 'From the beginning of the created world' does not mean 'from the beginning of created existence', for much existed before men and women came into existence: but, from the time when God was creating, at the end of which man and woman were made, each in a true sense incomplete without the other: neither male nor female is self-sufficient for the carrying on of the human race. See Gen. 2: 24.
7. After 'mother', 'and shall cleave to his wife' is probably added from Genesis and Matthew: but in any case a new relationship has been formed, closer than that between parent and child: husband and wife are 'fused into' one flesh, practically one 'person'. So to attempt to sever this union is to offend not only against human society, but against God, its originator.
10. Cf. 4: 34. The disciples could not feel sure that our Lord meant exactly what He said, without exception: they needed a private explanation. Our Lord does but emphasize His doctrine.

12. And if the wife shall put away her husband and be married to another, she committeth adultery.

Children: 13–16
(Matt. 19: 13–15; Luke 18: 15–17)

13. And they brought to him young children, that he might touch them. And the disciples rebuked them that brought them.
14. Whom when Jesus saw, he was much displeased and saith to them: Suffer the little children to come unto me and forbid them not; for of such is the kingdom of God.
15. Amen I say to you, whosoever shall not receive the kingdom of God as a little child shall not enter into it.

---

12. Yet this verse provides a difficulty. A Jewish woman could not repudiate her husband: the idea did not suggest itself (the case of Herodias was all the more shocking): but Roman and Egyptian women could, and it is possible that Gentile laxity was infecting also the Jews. There was a general weakening of morality. Our Lord tries not only to bring back Jewish marriage-principles to the level of the law of Moses, but to the original purity of God's institution. But see Notes on Matthew 19: 9; cf. 5: 32.
13. 'Children': παιδίον means children from 8 days old to 12 years: St. Luke's βρέφος means babies. The disciples may have thought that our Lord's doctrine was too important for time to be wasted in speaking to those who could not understand it—unaware of their own slowness of intelligence.
14. Our Lord was angry at this. 'Such as these', (τοιούτων): not merely 'these' (τούτων): that is, those of simple, docile spirit. Does the sentence mean: 'The Kingdom of God consists of those like these' or 'belongs to . . .'?
15. Anyhow, it is the simple who accept Christ's doctrine; therefore His Kingdom consists of them. To 'receive' the Kingdom is unusual. But not only is the Kingdom the place that you enter; it is a gift that you receive. Children run to those they recognize and love.

99

16. And embracing them and laying his hands upon them, he blessed them.

Riches and Renunciation: 17–31
(Matt. 19: 16–30; Luke 18: 18–30)

17. And when he was gone forth into the way, a certain man, running up and kneeling before him, asked him: Good Master, what shall I do that I may receive life everlasting?

18. And Jesus said to him: Why callest thou me good? None is good but one, that is God.

19. Thou knowest the commandments: *Do not commit adultery, do not kill, do not steal, bear not false witness, do no fraud, honour thy father and mother.*

20. But he answe ing, said to him: Master, all these things I have observed from my youth.

21. And Jesus, looking on him, loved him and said to him: One thing is wanting unto thee. Go, sell whatsoever thou hast and give to the

---

16. St Mark says that He kissed them, as well as blessing them as had been asked.

17. St Matthew says he was young; St Luke, a leading man in the synagogue. For 'receive', read 'inherit'. He was an enthusiast—he ran, he knelt: he exclaimed at the goodness of this Rabbi—had he watched our Lord with the children?

18. Either our Lord meant: 'You have seen only what is exterior —my works, my behaviour: you do not really know me yet'; or, 'good' is more nearly 'kind'—he had seen our Lord with the children, and thought he would have an easy answer; but our Lord shows Himself *exacting*.

19. 'Do no fraud' ($\mu\grave{\eta}$ $\mathring{\alpha}\pi o\sigma\tau\epsilon\rho\acute{\eta}\sigma\eta s$) is in Mark only, and not in the written text of the Law. As so often, we find that Mark is not 'bookish': he writes as one who had heard St Peter *speaking*—almost as if he were speaking himself.

20. He evidently expects our Lord to suggest something extra, in view of reaching perfection—but, he did not foresee how much it would be.

poor: and thou shalt have treasure in heaven. And come, follow me.

22. Who being struck sad at that saying, went away sorrowful: for he had great possessions.

23. And Jesus looking round about, saith to his disciples: How hardly shall they that have riches enter into the kingdom of God!

24. And the disciples were astonished at his words. But Jesus again answering, saith to them: Children, how hard is it for them that trust in riches to enter into the kingdom of God?

25. It is easier for a camel to pass through the eye of a needle than for a rich man to enter into the kingdom of God.

26. Who wondered the more, saying among themselves: Who then can be saved?

---

21. Our Lord 'looks him in the eyes' (ἐμβλέψας), and loves him for his innocence (we must not think the young man had been boasting!), and so, wished yet better things for him. 'Go' (Ὕπαγε), 'Off with you!' followed by δεῦρο, 'Hither!' 'Be off—but return!' That is, our Lord told him to go away *then*, but hoped he would return.

22. Στυγνάσας: 'scowling' might be too strong: but St Peter remembered the very expression of his face.

23. 'Looking round' at them all—a favourite expression of St Mark's, he uses it 6 times, St Luke once; St Matthew, never.

24. 'Very astonished': for the Old Testament had taught that 'riches', worldly prosperity, were just what the virtuous would obtain. 'Those that trust in riches' seems a very good explanation of the bald 'riches', since riches are not bad in themselves. Still, they usually breed self-sufficiency and contempt of the poorer. Cf. 'The *love* of money is the root of every kind of (not "all") evil': Tim. 6: 10.

25. A not uncommon proverb. The Talmud speaks too of an elephant passing through a needle's eye. There is no need to translate κάμηλος as a 'ship's cable', though this was often suggested in antiquity, for κάμηλος could also mean that; nor are there grounds for thinking that a narrow gate in the walls of Jerusalem is referred to.

27. And Jesus looking on them, saith: With men it is impossible; but not with God. For all things are possible with God.

28. And Peter began to say unto him: Behold, we have left all things and have followed thee.

29. Jesus answering, said: Amen I say to you, there is no man who hath left house or brethren or sisters or father or mother or children or lands, for my sake and for the gospel,

30. Who shall not receive an hundred times as much, now in this time; houses and brethren and sisters and mothers and children and lands, with persecutions: and in the world to come life everlasting.

31. But many that are first shall be last: and the last, first.

---

27. 'Fixing his eyes upon them'—the rich *can* be saved, but not without God's help.

28. Peter 'began' to say to him: St Mark omits St Matthew's words: 'What then will there be for us?' Possibly, as time went on, St Peter felt this was rather a 'pushing' thing to say? Nor does St Mark record our Lord's answer that they (the Apostles) should sit on twelve thrones, judging the tribes of Israel: this might have been unintelligible or distasteful to his Gentile readers.

29. 'The Gospel': St Mark uses this word thus 8 times: St Matthew 4; St. Luke never.

30. The reward is to be given, partly, in this life; very likely it implies that the true, self-renouncing Christian will find all and more than all he wants even on the material plane—no friendships are so numerous and lasting as those he forms: but also, St Mark (and only he) adds 'with persecutions' and the history of the Church proves him right.

31. This might mean that the roles will be inverted, and the despised Apostles shall be first, hereafter; and e.g. the Pharisees, last: in this case δέ the Greek word, here translated 'but', is practically 'and', i.e. those who now rank first—the Pharisees—shall be last; the poor Apostles, first. If, however, it makes a strong contrast, '*but*', the sense will be that the Apostles, who *are* and shall be (if they persevere) 'first', must

CHAPTER TEN

Again the Passion is Predicted: 32–34

(Matt. 20: 17–19; Luke 18: 31–34)

32. And they were in the way going up to Jerusalem: and Jesus went before them. And they were astonished and following were afraid. And taking again the twelve, he began to tell them the things that should befall him.

33. Saying: Behold we go up to Jerusalem, and the Son of man shall be betrayed to the chief priests and to the scribes and ancients. And they shall condemn him to death and shall deliver him to the Gentiles.

34. And they shall mock him and spit on him and scourge him and kill him: and the third day he shall rise again.

The Sons of Zebedee: 35–45

(Matt. 20: 20–28; Luke 22: 25 ff.)

35. And James and John, the sons of Zebedee, come to him, saying: Master, we desire that whatsoever we shall ask, thou wouldst do it for us.

36. But he said to them: What would you that I should do for you?

---

be on their guard lest they fail; and, others, who seem hopeless, may find themselves 'first' after all. St Bede mentions Judas, and the Penitent Thief.

32. To 'go up' to Jerusalem was a regular turn of phrase, not only due to Jerusalem being on a high elevation. Our Lord went ahead, as though eager to reach His destination (cf. Luke 12: 50): the disciples were surprised at this: *others*, following, were downright frightened. Our Lord had been spending time across the Jordan, precisely because He foresaw and foretold what would happen to Him in Jerusalem, yet here He was, hurrying ahead, and as it were dragging the others after Him. This third prophecy of the Passion is much more detailed than the previous ones. Luke 18: 34, emphasizes that, even so, the disciples did not understand.

35. St Matthew shows their mother as making the petition. 'We desire . . .': rather, 'we demand': 'it is our will'.

103

37. And they said: Grant to us that we may sit, one on thy right hand and the other on thy left hand, in thy glory.

38. And Jesus said to them: You know not what you ask. Can you drink of the chalice that I drink of or be baptized with the baptism wherewith I am baptized?

39. But they said to him: We can. And Jesus saith to them: You shall indeed drink of the chalice that I drink of; and with the baptism wherewith I am baptized you shall be baptized.

40. But to sit on my right hand or on my left is not mine to give to you, but to them for whom it is prepared.

41. And the ten, hearing it, began to be much displeased at James and John.

42. But Jesus calling them, saith to them: You know that they who seem to rule over the Gentiles lord it over them: and their princes have power over them.

---

37. Evidently they realize that He is Messias, but not that the Passion must precede the glory. If they recall the 'twelve thrones' (Matt. 19: 28), St Mark at any rate has not mentioned that promise.

38. 'Chalice', i.e. destiny: the 'Cup' in the Old Testament could contain sweetness or bitterness (Ps. 22: 5; 115: 4; Is. 51: 17, 22, etc.): but 'can you . . .?' indicates that the Cup would be hard to drink. As for 'Baptism', in the Old Testament and in Greek and Latin literature, the idea of being 'plunged in', 'overwhelmed by' a flood of sorrows, etc., is quite common. They say, too boldly: 'We can' and our Lord agrees that they shall indeed share His destiny. James was killed by Herod Agrippa about A.D. 44: tradition held that John died a natural death.

40. The Greek omits 'to you': our Lord, while on earth, cannot ever anticipate His Father's decree.

42. Our Lord calls the indignant Ten and explains what Christian humility entails, and also explains His own death. 'Those who appear to govern pagan nations', either because their power is not really theirs, but is God-given: or, 'who are

43. But it is not so among you: but whosoever will be greater shall be your minister.

44. And whosoever will be first among you shall be the servant of all.

45. For the Son of man also is not come to be ministered unto: but to minister and to give his life a redemption for many.

Bartimaeus: 46–52

(Matt. 20: 29–34; Luke 18: 33–43)

46. And they came to Jericho. And as he went out of Jericho with his disciples and a very great multitude, Bartimeus the blind man, the son of Timeus, sat by the way side begging.

---

recognized as rulers', i.e. by their subjects. 'Lord it over them' ($\kappa\alpha\tau\alpha\kappa\upsilon\rho\iota\epsilon\acute{\upsilon}o\upsilon\sigma\iota\nu$) and have 'power over' ($\kappa\alpha\tau\epsilon\xi\upsilon\sigma\iota\acute{\alpha}\zeta\upsilon\sigma\iota\nu$): grind them *down* with their arbitrary rule.

44. Hence the papal title *servus servorum Dei*.

45. *Even* the Son of Man 'came'—and is therefore Messias: yet He asks but to serve. Moreover, He will give His life not just as a witness to His own loyalty to truth and right, but as a 'ransom' for 'many'. This does not mean, 'not for all', but 'one life for many lives'. 'For', $\dot{\alpha}\nu\tau\acute{\iota}$, means 'instead of': 'For the sake of' would have required $\dot{\upsilon}\pi\acute{\epsilon}\rho$. See 1 Tim. 2: 6: 'Who gave himself as a ransom for the sake of all.'

46. Jericho was a sort of holiday resort, 1,200 feet below sea-level. Jerusalem was 2,500 above sea-level. St Mark and St Matthew say that the miracle occurred as they were leaving the city; St Luke as they were approaching it. It is possible that this discrepancy is due to there having been *two* Jerichos, the ancient city, and the new one built alongside of it by Herod the Great. The miracle then will have taken place as they left the older town and approached the new. St Matthew speaks of *two* blind men, as he does of two demoniacs at Gadara. Perhaps one was known to St Mark but not to St Matthew or St Luke, who do not name him.

47. Who when he heard that it was Jesus of Nazareth, began to cry out and to say: Jesus, Son of David, have mercy on me.

48. And many rebuked him, that he might hold his peace; but he cried a great deal the more: Son of David, have mercy on me.

49. And Jesus, standing still, commanded him to be called. And they call the blind man, saying to him: Be of better comfort. Arise, he calleth thee.

50. Who casting off his garment leaped up and came to him.

51. And Jesus answering, said to him: What wilt thou that I should do to thee? And the blind man said to him: Rabboni. That I may see.

52. And Jesus saith to him: Go thy way. Thy faith hath made thee whole. And immediately he saw and followed him in the way.

---

47. 'Son of David' was the most usual title of the Messias: the blind man, having heard about Jesus, must have felt sure that this was He who should open the eyes of the blind (Is. 61: 1).

48. 'Several' tried to silence him—not as objecting to the title, but to so unsuitable a clamour. But when they saw that Jesus stood still and summoned him, their sympathy swung round and they encouraged him.

51. Our Lord's question served to elicit the man's faith and make it clear that he was asking for a miracle, not money.

52. Ὕπαγε cf. 21: 'Be off!' But the man followed Jesus.

CHAPTER ELEVEN

Palm Sunday: *The Entry into Jerusalem*: 1–10
(Matt. 21: 1–11; Luke 19: 29–45; John 12: 1, 12–19)

1. And when they were drawing near to Jerusalem and to Bethania, at the mount of Olives, he sendeth two of his disciples,
2. And saith to them: Go into the village that is over against you, and immediately at your coming in thither, you shall find a colt tied, upon which no man yet hath sat. Loose him and bring him.
3. And if any man shall say to you: What are you doing? Say ye that the Lord hath need of him. And immediately he will let him come hither.

---

1. We should read: 'towards Bethphage and Bethania, to the Mount of Olives.' If our Lord took the shortest but steepest way from Jericho He would have passed Bethany to His left, on the eastern slope of the Mount of Olives, having Bethphage in front of Him near the summit.
2. The village was probably, therefore, Bethphage; but the site of these two villages is not quite certain. Pierced stones, or metal rings on the wall, were quite commonly used for tying up animals. 'Colt'; in classical Greek πῶλος would be a young horse; in Palestine, an ass's colt, the usual way of riding (cf. Gen. 32: 15, etc.). No one yet had mounted the one they were to find, so it could in no way have been 'profaned'.
3. 'Lord' (κύριος), does not mean much more than 'master', save doubtless in the mind of the evangelist: also it is clear that our Lord was viewing His entry into Jerusalem as 'Messianic'. He was careful to imply that the colt would be given back: here was no *despotic* act.

4. And going their way, they found the colt tied before the gate without, in the meeting of two ways. And they loose him.

5. And some of them that stood there said to them: What do you loosing the colt?

6. Who said to them as Jesus had commanded them. And they let him go with them.

7. And they brought the colt to Jesus. And they lay their garments on him: and he sat upon him.

8. And many spread their garments in the way: and others cut down boughs from the trees and strewed them in the way.

9. And they that went before and they that followed cried, saying: *Hosanna: Blessed is he that cometh in the name of the Lord.*

10. *Blessed be the kingdom of our father David that cometh: Hosanna in the highest.*

---

4. 'Before the gate without'; 'At the door, in the street'. Ἐπὶ τοῦ ἀμφόδου need not mean more than in the 'street': the Vulgate *bivium*, 'at the meeting of two ways' is an accurate translation but untrue to usage.

5. 'Some of the by-standers': in a small village everyone knew everyone else, and was interested in what went on.

7. The colt naturally had no saddle as yet; hence the clothes placed on it: but distinguished persons often spread cloaks on their mounts even though saddled.

8. To spread clothes on someone's path was a mark of great honour (4 Kings 9: 13): the 'boughs' (στιβάδες) were twigs, probably of olives: compare flowers thrown before the Monstrance in processions.

9. Young men took the lead; then came our Lord doubtless surrounded by the disciples; women and older men followed.

10. 'Hosanna' probably means, literally, 'Save us!' but 'Save us in the Highest' would be strange: it had become simply an acclamation. 'That of our father, David, the Kingdom that is arriving': the Messias was expected to restore that Davidic Kingdom. 'Blessed *be* he that cometh.' All this is from Psalm 117, a processional psalm. The shout of Hosanna is to reach

CHAPTER ELEVEN

Our Lord Inspects the Temple: 11

11. And he entered into Jerusalem, into the temple: and having viewed all things round about, when now the eventide was come, he went out to Bethania with the twelve.

The Barren Fig Tree (i): 12–14
(Matt. 21: 18–19)

12. And the next day when they came out from Bethania, he was hungry.

---

as high as heaven. By this 'entry' our Lord fulfilled the prophecy of Zach. 9: 9. ('Behold, the King cometh unto thee . . . meek, riding upon an ass, even a colt, the foal of an ass.') But the rabbis themselves discussed how the Messias *could* come in so insignificant a way. We must not picture this event like a modern royal procession, through streets carefully emptied and guarded. The valleys round Jerusalem were already beginning to seethe with the paschal pilgrims: there was a universal uproar: our Lord on the colt will hardly have been raised above the crowds: camels and probably Roman officers on horses would have been much more noticeable. He entered indeed as Messias, but not as the Messias they were expecting: He entered knowing that He was moving straight to His redeeming death.

11. Our Lord does indeed enter the temple, but not to make a Messianic demonstration: He inspects the scene, but, since it was late, He did nothing at the time: He returned to Bethany where, we see from John 11, and below, 14: 3, that He had friends, Martha and Mary and Lazarus.

12. If our Lord was really hungry, why had He not eaten before leaving Bethany? St John Chrysostom suggests that the disciples *assumed* He must be hungry, since He approached a fig tree to see if possibly (εἰ ἄρα) He might find something (to eat) on it: but He found nothing but leaves, since it was not yet the season for figs. It must be definitely said that at the end of March or the beginning of April fig trees could be in leaf, especially on the eastern slopes of Mount Olivet where

13. And when he had seen afar off a fig tree having leaves, he came, if perhaps he might find any thing on it. And when he was come to it, he found nothing but leaves. For it was not the time for figs.

14. And answering he said to it: May no man hereafter eat fruit of thee any more for ever! And his disciples heard it.

The Cleansing of the Temple: 15–19
(Matt. 21: 12–17; Luke 19: 45–48)

15. And they came to Jerusalem. And when he was entered into the temple, he began to cast out them that sold and bought in the temple: and overthrew the tables of the moneychangers and the chairs of them that sold doves.

16. And he suffered not that any man should carry a vessel through the temple.

17. And he taught, saying to them: Is it not written: *My house shall be called the house of prayer to all nations, but you have made it a den of thieves?*

trees may begin to grow green a fortnight earlier than in Jerusalem: but it is most unusual that eatable figs should have been found so early. Our Lord then said: 'May no man ever any more eat fruit from thee.' (See below, on verse 20.)

15. The great Court of the Gentiles had become a sort of 'oriental bazaar'. Oxen, lambs, salt, wine, oil were needed for sacrifices: the vendors of these had 'shops' arranged under the colonnades. Doves, which the poorer pilgrims offered, were sold by men sitting here and there on chairs. The moneychangers were necessary since only Jewish money might be used in the temple, at any rate for the annual temple tribute of half a shekel, and pilgrims might arrive with only Roman or Greek money: the moneychanger demanded a small commission, κόλλυβος: here was every danger of cheating and wrangling.

16. Only St Mark adds that Jesus would not allow the temple-court to be used as a short cut, which they would more readily do if they had to carry something heavy, like a wine-jar.

18. Which when the chief priests and the scribes had heard, they sought how they might destroy him. For they feared him, because the whole multitude was in admiration at his doctrine.

19. And when evening was come, he went forth out of the city.

The Fig Tree (ii): 20–21
(Matt. 21: 19b–30)

20. And when they passed by in the morning they saw the fig tree dried up from the roots.

---

17. Our Lord quotes Is. 56: 7, who says that proselytes from 'all nations' shall come to Jerusalem, and the temple would be a house of prayer for them: and in Jer. 7: 11, the Lord asks if indeed His house, over which His name is called, is to be a den of thieves. Even this 'outer court' should have been consecrated to worship: it could never have been quiet, given the bellowing of the victims and the braying of the trumpets and the general tumult proper to any oriental crowd: but at least the financial transactions—especially if dishonest—should not have taken place there.

18. For the first time, we find the chief priests (who ought to have kept order in the temple) and the Scribes, acting together, the more remarkably, because the great priestly families were mostly Sadducees. Possibly the 'shops' paid rent to the temple authorities.

19. Jesus did not feel safe in the City at night. Probably they returned to Bethany.

20. St Matthew describes the withering as following immediately upon the 'curse': an example of how the Evangelists can describe an identical event in somewhat different ways (see also on the Cleansing of the Temple, which St Matthew and St Luke place immediately after the triumphal entry into the City). This incident is best described as a 'parable in action'; that is, our Lord would have wished His Nation and the Holy City to have been rich in fruits of virtue: instead, He found a fine display of foliage—the crowds of pilgrims; the constant

21. And Peter remembering, said to him: Rabbi, behold the fig tree which thou didst curse is withered away.

Faith: Forgiveness: 22–26

(Matt. 21: 21–22; cf. 17: 20; 6: 14; Luke 17: 6)

22. And Jesus answering, saith to them: Have the faith of God.
23. Amen I say to you that whosoever shall say to this mountain, Be thou removed and be cast into the sea, and shall not stagger in his heart, but believe that whatsoever he saith shall be done; it shall be done unto him.
24. Therefore I say unto you, all things, whatsoever you ask when ye pray, believe that you shall receive: and they shall come unto you.
25. And when you shall stand to pray, forgive, if you have aught against any man: that your Father also, who is in heaven, may forgive you your sins.

---

sacrifices; the Pasch being turned into a money-making affair. Naturally our Lord knew quite well that the fig tree as such could not yet produce fruits: but the leafy, fruitless tree stood as a valuable symbol for the sterile cult of the Jews: His condemnation was seen effective in the case of Jerusalem, in so short a time to be demolished and worship there, even external, to cease.

22. 'Faith of God', i.e. in God; 'objective genitive': e.g. *amor patris*, love for a father.
23. The expression was proverbial. 'This mountain' was Olivet, from which the Dead Sea could be seen. Cf. 'If I have all faith, so as to move mountains' (1 Cor. 13: 2). 'Stagger' (διακρίνεσθαι) really means 'to judge this way and that', i.e. to decide: but in the New Testament it has come to mean 'to hesitate', i.e. between two decisions (cf. Acts 1: 20; Rom. 4: 20; James 1: 6, etc.). The prayer which is infallibly granted is that which is prayed with full faith in God (and therefore betokens a will to ask only what God wills).
25. But our faith must be accompanied by charity even towards those who have offended us. St Mark does not quote the

26. But if you will not forgive, neither will your Father that is in heaven forgive you your sins.

'By What Authority?': 27–33
(Matt. 21: 23–27; Luke 20: 1–8)

27. And they come again to Jerusalem. And when he was walking in the temple, there come to him the chief priests and the scribes and the ancients.

28. And they say to him: By what authority dost thou these things? And who hath given thee this authority that thou shouldst do these things?

29. And Jesus answering, said to them: I will also ask you one word. And answer you me: and I will tell you by what authority I do these things.

30. The baptism of John, was it from heaven or from men? Answer me.

31. But they thought with themselves, saying: If we say, From heaven; he will say, Why then did you not believe him?

32. If we say, From men, we fear the people. For all men counted John that he was a prophet indeed.

33. And they answering, say to Jesus: We know not. And Jesus answering, saith to them: Neither do I tell you by what authority I do these things.

'Our Father', but its governing idea is perceived here. Cf. Matt. 6: 14; 17: 20. Verse 26 is not found in the best MSS.

27. Our Lord is approached by representatives of the three groups composing the Sanhedrin (8: 31). 'These things', ($\tau\alpha\hat{\upsilon}\tau\alpha$) must refer to the scene in the temple: our Lord had acted as though *He*, not the temple-police, were responsible for what went on there. Cf. Acts 4: 7: 'By what power and in what name (do you act thus)?'

30. 'Answer me!' Typical of our Lord's blunt way of speaking, as St Mark reports Him.

31, 32. They do not think of answering according to their conscience or conviction, but only what is opportune. We should read: '"From man?"—they feared the people!' This leaving a

sentence unfinished is again in St Mark's abrupt style. Our
Lord suggests, while refusing a direct answer, that John's
authority did come from God, since he witnessed to
righteousness at the expense of his own life. And further,
that His own authority came from heaven, albeit He too was
to die.

CHAPTER TWELVE

The Parable of the Vineyard: 1–12

(Matt. 21: 33–46; Luke 20: 9–19)

1. And he began to speak to them in parables: A certain man planted a vineyard and made a hedge about it and dug a place for the winevat and built a tower and let it to husbandmen: and went into a far country.

2. And at the season he sent to the husbandmen a servant to receive of the husbandmen of the fruit of the vineyard.

---

1. 'Parables': this need not mean 'several parables', but a special sort of instruction. This parable goes nearer than most to being an allegory: but even so we should not seek for a particular meaning appropriate to each detail—thus, the vineyard is certainly the People, but we need not suppose that the 'wall' means the Law, fencing them off from the Gentiles, etc. Every vineyard had a stone wall round it, and a stone tower so that an eye might be kept on marauders, whether beasts or men. The wine-vat (ὑπολήνιον) consisted of a saucer-shaped stone under the actual place where the grapes were trodden: thence the juice ran through a hollow channel into a larger receptacle, also hewn in the rock. All this description is taken from Is. 5: 1–7, save that there the whole people is guilty; here, the governing class whose duty it was to guide the people spiritually. 'Went into a far country', 'Ἀπεδήμησεν; 'went abroad', as we might say.

2. God is not absent, but invisible: He expects to receive His dues from those in whose charge He entrusts His possessions. 'But if the owner of the vineyard had gone far off, how could he expect to have the wine sent to him?' His agent could take

115

3. Who, having laid hands on him, beat him and sent him away empty.
4. And again he sent to them another servant: and him they wounded in the head and used him reproachfully.
5. And again he sent another, and him they killed: and many others, of whom some they beat, and others they killed.
6. Therefore, having yet one son, most dear to him, he also sent him unto them last of all, saying: They will reverence my son.
7. But the husbandmen said one to another: This is the heir. Come let us kill him and the inheritance shall be ours.
8. And laying hold on him, they killed him and cast him out of the vineyard.
9. What therefore will the lord of the vineyard do? He will come and destroy those husbandmen and will give the vineyard to others.

---

what the husbandmen owed, in kind, and sell it, and transmit the money to his master, or 'bank' it. 'At the season' ($\tau\hat{\omega}\ \kappa\alpha\iota\rho\hat{\omega}$) 'at the proper time'.

3. $\Delta\acute{\epsilon}\rho\epsilon\iota\nu$: Except as slang 'to tan', in the sense to 'beat', 'mal-treat', occurs only in the New Testament.
4. 'Wounded in the head' ($\acute{\epsilon}\kappa\epsilon\phi\alpha\lambda\acute{\iota}\omega\sigma\alpha\nu$) probably means:
5. 'beat him on the head'. The third is killed: the Jews had many legends about the death of the prophets: thus St Jerome says that they held Jeremias to have been killed in Egypt; Isaias, to have been sawn asunder. Our Lord Himself says that Zacharias was stoned to death (Matt. 23: 35; Acts 7: 52). St Mark wishes us to realize how long-suffering God is: how, as it were, He hopes against hope that His people will be converted.
6. 'Yet he still had one, a son, his well-beloved.'
7. 'They' ($\acute{\epsilon}\kappa\epsilon\hat{\iota}\nu\sigma\iota$): almost, 'those wretched husband-men . . .' It was illogical to assume that if the legal heir was got rid of, the vineyard would be *theirs*. The point is, that by rejecting the true Messias, the Jewish rulers were signing their own death-warrant. They might kill the heir, and get rid of his dead body; but they in their turn would be got rid of and others would replace them.

10. And have you not read this scripture, *The stone which the builders rejected, the same is made the head of the corner:*

11. *By the Lord has this been done, and it is wonderful in our eyes.*

12. And they sought to lay hands on him: but they feared the people. For they knew that he spoke this parable to them. And leaving him, they went their way.

Tribute to Cæsar: 13–17

(Matt. 22: 15–22; Luke 20: 20–26)

13. And they sent to him some of the Pharisees and of the Herodians: that they should catch him in his words.

14. Who coming, say to him: Master, we know that thou art a true speaker and carest not for any man; for thou regardest not the person of men, but teachest the way of God in truth. Is it lawful to give tribute to Cæsar? Or shall we not give it?

---

10. Ps. 107: 22, 23, was generally held to be Messianic: but the metaphor is changed and the meaning of the parable enlarged: the builders reject a certain stone—and that very stone becomes the 'corner-stone', i.e. the all-important stone linking and supporting two walls of a building: cf. Eph. 2: 20.

12. They realized that he had spoken the parable 'at' them. *They* were the wicked husbandmen, to be supplanted. In Luke, more artistic but less simple, there are only three messengers, representing the older, the more recent prophets, and the Son.

13. 'Catch' ($\dot{a}\gamma\rho\epsilon\acute{u}\epsilon\iota\nu$): 'catch in the hunt': but St Matthew uses the word $\pi\alpha\gamma\iota\delta\epsilon\acute{u}\epsilon\iota\nu$, to catch in a net: 'in his word' ($\lambda\acute{o}\gamma\omega$): by means of their word: or, possibly, 'in His answer'. The Pharisees were hostile to the Roman rule, but did not show this openly: the Herodians had a prince of the house of Herod, but maintained good relations with Rome.

14. They approach our Lord with elaborate courtesy, well aware that He was no intriguer or likely to succumb to 'human respect': 'regarding not the person of men' ($\beta\lambda\acute{e}\pi\epsilon\iota\nu$ $\epsilon\dot{\iota}s$ $\pi\rho\acute{o}\sigma\omega\pi\sigma\nu$ $\dot{a}\nu\theta\rho\acute{\omega}\pi\omega\nu$) means simply 'to regard human con-

15. Who knowing their wiliness, saith to them: Why tempt you me? Bring me a penny that I may see it.

16. And they brought it him. And he saith to them: Whose is this image and inscription? They say to him, Cæsar's.

17. And Jesus answering, said to them: Render therefore to Cæsar the things that are Cæsar's and to God the things that are God's. And they marvelled at him.

---

ventions'. 'The way of God': the 'way' was a well-known expression—God is man's goal; the question is, how best to walk towards Him. In the Acts (9: 2; 19: 9, 23; 24: 14, 22) the 'Way' is Christian doctrine. The Greek is far more vivid than the Vulgate. 'Is it lawful to give? or not? Are we to give, or not give?' The Greek word for 'tribute', κῆνσος, is unexpected. Elsewhere it is always φόρος. *Census* means, rather, the examination of a person's status and possessions. It is not really an example of St Mark's 'latinisms', for it was transliterated both into Greek and Aramaic. They thought that if our Lord said 'No' (as Judas of Galilee had said at the time of the census of Quirinius), He would be regarded by the Roman authority as a rebel: if He said 'Yes', He would seem to be unfaithful to Jewish nationalism.

15. The *denarius* was a silver coin—as it were a shilling. See on 6: 37. The Jews were allowed to coin small bronze coins, bearing some stamp such as a palm, or vine-leaf: thus their susceptibilities regarding the portrayal of the human form were unoffended. However the tetrarch Philip and Herod Agrippa did not hesitate to print the face of the emperor on their bronze coinage. The effigy will have been that of Augustus, or of Tiberius, 'son of the Divine Augustus'. Not only did the Jews accept the Roman government, but in Judea had even asked for a Roman procurator in preference to being ruled by the tyrannous descendant of Herod the Great:

17. Let them therefore give to Cæsar what belonged to him, but not, on that account, neglect the far higher duty of obeying the Law of God.

Marriage and Human Resurrection: 18–27

(Matt. 22: 23–33; Luke 20: 27–38)

18. And there came to him the Sadducees, who say there is no resurrection. And they asked him, saying:

19. Master, Moses wrote unto us that if any man's brother die and leave his wife behind him and leave no children, his brother should take his wife and raise up seed to his brother.

20. Now there were seven brethren: and the first took a wife and died leaving no issue.

21. And the second took her and died: and neither did he leave any issue. And the third in like manner.

22. And the seven all took her in like manner and did not leave issue. Last of all the woman also died.

23. In the resurrection therefore, when they shall rise again, whose wife shall she be of them? For the seven had her to wife.

24. And Jesus answering, saith to them: Do ye not therefore err, because you know not the scriptures nor the power of God?

25. For when they shall rise again from the dead, they shall neither marry, nor be married, but are as the angels in heaven.

---

18. The Sadducees were a 'party' (Acts 5: 17) closely connected with the priesthood. Not only did they try to affect Hellenistic culture, but (Acts 23: 8) they admitted neither resurrection, nor angel, nor spirit.

19. The reference is to Deut. 25: 5, which is much less absolute inasmuch as Moses speaks only of brothers who live together, or in the same district. The very nature of the 'case' put forward shows how insincere, if not frivolous, was the Sadducees' argument.

25. Our Lord does not discuss the *manner* of the resurrection, nor the nature of angels, but implies that in the 'future life' there will be no need to prolong family life as here. Both souls and angels are living on a different plane. It is in this matter that they misunderstood the power of God, who is able to raise men to life after bodily death, which no human agency can do. He then refers to the Scriptures and in particular to Ex. 3: 6;

26. And as concerning the dead that they rise again have you not read in the book of Moses, how in the bush God spoke to him, saying: *I am the God of Abraham and the God of Isaac and the God of Jacob?*

27. He is not the God of the dead but of the living. You therefore do greatly err.

The Two Commandments: 28–34
(Matt. 22: 34–40; Luke 10: 23–28)

28. And there came one of the scribes that had heard them reasoning together, and seeing that he had answered them well, asked him which was the first commandment of all.

---

the Sadducees certainly admitted the authority of the Pentateuch even if, it is usually thought, they discarded the rest of the Old Testament. Our Lord alludes to the section of the Book of Exodus called 'On the Bush'. Strictly speaking, in the passage referred to, God says only that He is the same God as the God whom Abraham, Isaac and Jacob worshipped and with whom He made His covenant. The normal Jewish view of immortality had been, and probably still was, very vague: souls survived in Sheol, but with a poor, imperfect life. Our Lord suggests that it is unthinkable that God should abandon those who had loved and served Him to this sort of half-life: somehow, He would withdraw such souls from the gloom of Sheol into full life with Himself. Cf. Ps. 16: 8; 49: 15; 73: 32, etc.

27. Our Lord, who began His interview so courteously—'Might it not be that you are going wrong through not knowing the Scriptures?' (24) ends with two words only, like hammer-strokes: πολὺ πλανᾶσθε, 'You are utterly wrong.'

28. In Mark, the Scribe is clearly well-disposed: even in Matthew, 'testing him' need not prove ill-will: St Matthew says, too, that he was sent by the Pharisees who heard that Jesus had silenced the Sadducees, which must have delighted them. Perhaps not a few Pharisees would have welcomed new proofs of the 'orthodoxy' of our Lord.

29. And Jesus answered him: The first commandment of all is, *Hear, O Israel: the Lord thy God is one God.*

30. *And thou shalt love the Lord thy God with thy whole heart and with thy whole soul and with thy whole mind and with thy whole strength.* This is the first commandment.

31. And the second is like to it: *Thou shalt love thy neighbour as thyself.* There is no other commandment greater than these.

32. And the scribe said to him: Well, Master, thou hast said in truth that there is one God and there is no other besides him.

33. And that he should be loved with the whole heart and with the whole understanding and with the whole soul and with the whole strength. And to love one's neighbour as one's self is a greater thing than all holocausts and sacrifices.

34. And Jesus seeing that he had answered wisely, said to him: Thou art not far from the kingdom of God. And no man after that durst ask him any question.

---

30. The quotation is from Deut. 6: 4 where however the word 'heart' probably stands for intelligence; 'soul', for feelings and emotions (not that we can always control these); 'mind' means 'thoughts' and adds nothing to 'heart': and we are to do this with all the energy that is ours. The Jews took Deut. 6: 8 literally, and wrote out the above words and placed them in a sort of satchel (φυλακτήριον: a keeping-place) and wore them on their foreheads.

31. The Greek was simply: 'The second is this': it is from Lev. 19: 18; we may doubt if 'neighbour' there means more than fellow-Hebrews: our Lord may not have been the first to join these two texts—so far apart!—together; for St Luke (10: 27) shows the Lawyer who interrogated our Lord on the subject doing so: but Luke may, however, have displaced the subject in order to lead up to the parable of the Good Samaritan.

32–34. These verses are in Mark only.

The 'Son of David': 35–37

(Matt. 22: 41–45; Luke 20: 41–44)

35. And Jesus answering, said, teaching in the temple: How do the scribes say that Christ is the son of David?

36. For David himself saith by the Holy Ghost: *The Lord said to my Lord: Sit on my right hand, until I make thy enemies thy foot-stool.*

37. David therefore himself calleth him Lord. And whence is he then his son? And a great multitude heard him gladly.

---

35. This seems to be a detached fragment, and does not do more than show that the Scribes are not true to their own principles (in fact, it is hard to suppose that these discontinuous episodes were all packed into three days of Holy Week). Everyone, Scribes and people, expected that the Messias would be of the House of David. But it was misleading to suppose that He would be *only* that, or that His chief task was to restore the Davidic Kingdom upon earth, even in an idealized form (Is. 11). Our Lord assumes that Ps. 109: 1, is (1) written by David, and (2) inspired. David therefore says: 'The LORD said to my Lord: Sit at my right hand, etc.' 'The LORD' represents the sacred Name of God Himself, which is usually written, in English letters, Yahweh. But 'my Lord' is 'Adonai'. There are therefore three persons concerned—David, who writes the Psalm: God: and the third, to whom God speaks, and whom David describes as his 'Lord'. This is recognized by all as meaning the Messias (in the New Testament, e.g. Acts 2: 34; 1 Cor. 15: 25; Eph. 1: 20–22, and often in Hebrews). Therefore, if the Messias is to descend from David (which is granted), *yet* he must be someone far higher than David, in fact, of a different nature, since no mere man is bidden by God to sit on His right hand.

37. One may doubt whether this means more than that the mass of the people *enjoyed* listening to this argumentation: repartee or refutations are always to the taste of the Oriental.

A Warning against Ostentation: 38–40
(Luke 20: 45, 47; Cf. Matt. 23: 1 ff.)

38. And he said to them in his doctrine: Beware of the scribes, who love to walk in long robes and to be saluted in the market-place,

39. And to sit in the first chairs in the synagogues and to have the highest places at suppers:

40. Who devour the houses of widows under the pretence of long prayer. These shall receive greater judgment.

'*The Widow's Mite*': 41–44
(Luke 21: 1–4)

41. And Jesus sitting over against the treasury, beheld how the people cast money into the treasury. And many that were rich cast in much.

42. And there came a certain poor widow: and she cast in two mites, which make a farthing.

---

38. Conservative-minded Jews still, it appears, wear long yellow or purple robes: the 'salute' is a low bow, accompanied by a still lower sweep of the right hand: then the more distinguished of the two admits the other to the kiss, on both cheeks. 'First seats—highest places', ($\pi\rho\omega\tau\text{o}\kappa\alpha\theta\epsilon\delta\rho\text{ί}\alpha\text{ι}$ and $\pi\rho\omega\tau\text{o}\kappa\lambda\iota\sigma\text{ί}\alpha\text{ι}$ occur only in the New Testament): it is not known how the places in dining-room or synagogue were settled.

40. Two separate faults are rebuked—they 'devour' the houses of defenceless widows (women depended almost wholly on male protection), less by asking alms than by their knowledge of the law: and, for a pretence they make long prayers. In Jewish writers themselves the tendency among the Pharisees to hypocrisy was fully recognized. (Cf. Matthew 6: 5.)

41. Our Lord must have passed into the Court of the Women where the openings into 'treasure' could be reached. The temple-area consisted first of the vast Court of the Gentiles, which anyone could enter: then the Court of the Women (beyond which they could not go): then the Court of Israel,

43. And calling his disciples together, he saith to them: Amen I say to you, this poor widow hath cast in more than all they who have cast into the treasury.

44. For all they did cast in of their abundance; but she of her want cast in all she had, even her whole living.

---

which men might enter: then the Court of the Priests where all that was needed for worship (the great brass altar, etc.) was placed: towards the west end of this was the Holy of Holies which was entered by the chief priest on the Day of Atonement only (Lev. 16). It is said that the offerings were placed in 13 tall receptacles called 'trumpets' under the colonnades: but the evidence for this cannot be checked. The coins were *lepta*, ($\lambda\epsilon\pi\tau\acute{a}$), i.e. half a quadrans, one sixteenth of the denarius (cf. p. 118): suitably translated 'farthing'. Aristotle had already mentioned the *moral* superiority of a smaller gift given from poverty over a larger gift given from opulence.

CHAPTER THIRTEEN

The 'Eschatological Discourse' (i): 1–2
(Matt. 24: 1–2; Luke 21: 5–6)

1. And as he was going out of the temple, one of his disciples said to him: Master, behold what manner of stones and what buildings are here.
2. And Jesus answering, said to him: Seest thou all these great buildings? There shall not be left a stone upon a stone, that shall not be thrown down.

The 'Eschatological Discourse' (ii): 3–8
(Matt. 24: 3–8; Luke 21: 7–11)

3. And as he sat on the mount of Olivet over against the temple, Peter and James and John and Andrew asked him apart:

---

1. Josephus says that the stones of the Temple itself were 25 cubits long, 8 high, and 12 in breadth: a cubit was about one and two-thirds feet. Some of the colossal stones of the foundations can still be seen and are even larger. Titus had meant to spare the Temple itself as a marvellous monument: but hearing it had been burnt down, demolished all that he could, temple-emplacement and city alike, A.D. 71.

2. The strong negative (οὐ μή) occurs twice in one sentence: it is shown that out of 60 times that this turn of speech occurs in the Gospels, 54 times it is in the mouth of our Lord. This may be an echo of the Aramaic He spoke; in any case it suggests the care of the Evangelists to keep as accurately as they could to His very words.

    All admit that in the following discourse there are two themes—the approaching destruction of Jerusalem, and the

4. Tell us, when shall these things be and what shall be the sign when all these things shall begin to be fulfilled?

5. And Jesus answering, began to say to them: Take heed lest any man deceive you.

6. For many shall come in my name saying, I am he: and they shall deceive many.

7. And when you shall hear of wars and rumours of wars, fear ye not. For such things must needs be: but the end is not yet.

8. For nation shall rise against nation and kingdom against kingdom: and there shall be earthquakes in divers places and famines. These things are the beginning of sorrows.

Second Advent of our Lord and the ending of the world. Sometimes our Lord speaks directly of the one and sometimes of the other. But often, in the spirit of all Hebrew prophecy, a greater, distant, or more spiritual truth or event is seen *in* something close at hand and material. Thus, looking at one bomb-shattered building, you might see *in* it the whole war, and the likelihood of further wars, and the destruction not only of one building but of a whole civilization—the end of one *sort* of world and the painful birth of another.

6. 'In my name' must here mean 'in the name that properly belongs to me', i.e. the Messias: it is unlikely that false Messiahs would appear claiming to be invested with the authority of our Lord Himself: the Apostles could speak with His authority, but never said: 'I am He!' It is certain that there were false Messiahs round about the time of the destruction of Jerusalem: doubtless they promised that the city would not be destroyed. The most famous one, Bar Kokhba, did not appear till much later.

7. 'Fear ye not': ($\theta\rho o\epsilon\hat{\iota}\sigma\theta\epsilon$) Do not be 'flustered', 'upset'.

8. It would be possible to make a catalogue of disasters occurring about this time; but it seems better to suppose that our Lord is using the 'prophetic dialect' and that all these disasters were symbolic of divine punishment—Is. 19: 2: 'Brother shall make war on brother, city against city, kingdom against

The 'Eschatological Discourse' (iii): 9–13

(Matt. 24: 9–14; Luke 21: 12–19. But cf. too Matt. 10: 17–21, 22a, 30,
22b; Luke 12: 11–12; and John 14: 16–26; 15: 21; 16: 2)

9. But look to yourselves. For they shall deliver you up to councils: and
in the synagogues you shall be beaten: and you shall stand before
governors and kings for my sake, for a testimony unto them.

---

kingdom': 4 Esdras 13: 30: 'Men shall plot to make war
on other men, state against state, place against place, people
against people and kingdom against kingdom': Is. 7: 21
(famines); 13: 13 (earthquakes) and so forth. The Hebrews
had a special sort of dialect for describing wars, idolatry,
imminent disasters, and our Lord speaks in the traditional
way. 'The beginning of sorrows' is a mistranslation. 'Ὠδῖναι
always means 'birth-pangs' (in Ps. 17: 5: 'birth-pangs of
death' is a violent paradox: what comes to life is—Death):
all these disasters lead up to a new birth of joy—a better
world.

Our Lord, having foretold the future in general, passes to
warn the disciples of what concerns them personally. But St
Matthew has already, in the places mentioned above, written
down not a little of what is said here, and even Luke 12:
11–12 is nearer Mark 13: 11, than in the strictly parallel
passage. It is then possible that St Mark combined parts of
various discourses: but more probably St Matthew and St
Luke, aware of what this great discourse was to contain,
found that parts of it came into their minds earlier too,
because of some association of ideas. (See Notes on those
Evangelists.)

9. The Sanhedrin of Jerusalem or inferior courts: here they
could be publicly flogged (2 Cor. 11: 24). 'Governors'
(ἡγέμονες), probably Roman procurators or other officials;
'kings', very likely the princes to whom, in Palestine as
elsewhere, the title of 'king' was permitted. The constancy
with which the disciples would endure such treatment should
be a strong witness to the genuineness of their mission.

10. And unto all nations the gospel must first be preached.

11. And when they shall lead you and deliver you up, be not thoughtful beforehand what you shall speak: but whatsoever shall be given you in that hour, that speak ye. For it is not you that speak, but the Holy Ghost.

12. And the brother shall betray his brother unto death, and the father his son; and children shall rise up against their parents and shall work their death.

13. And you shall be hated by all men for my name's sake. But he that shall endure unto the end, he shall be saved.

The 'Eschatological Discourse' (iv): 14–23
(Matt. 24: 15–25; Luke 21: 20–24)

14. And when you shall see the abomination of desolation, standing where it ought not (he that readeth let him understand): then let them that are in Judea flee unto the mountains.

---

10. St Luke omits this verse; St Matthew omits it in 10: 17–21, which is more like Mark than 24: 9–14 is: but there he places it after the verse parallel to Mark's 13. Some MSS. join 'and to all nations' to the preceding words—'a witness to them and to all nations', and continue; 'for first and foremost, the Gospel must be preached'. This in any case must be the meaning here; the reference cannot be to the end of the world, for that would make chaos of the context: we are still considering the state of things and the destiny of the Apostles *before* the downfall of Jerusalem.

11. 'Lead you'; i.e. arrest you and take you off. 'Be not thoughtful beforehand' ($\mu\grave{\eta}\ \pi\rho o\mu\epsilon\rho\iota\mu\nu\hat{a}\tau\epsilon$): do not 'pre-meditate' what you shall say: they were above all to trust to divine assistance: 'it is not *merely* you who will speak': not that the Holy Ghost will replace the human speaker, but He will speak through him.

12. Cf. especially Micheas, 7: 6.

13. It has been rightly pointed out that as in the earliest times *hatred* for Christianity was quite extraordinary, so in our times

15. And let him that is on the housetop not go down into the house nor enter therein to take any thing out of the house.

16. And let him that shall be in the field not turn back to take up his garment.

17. And woe to them that are with child and that give suck in those days.

---

it is the Catholic Church which beyond all other groups of Christians sets alight *hatred* among the enemies of religion.

14. 'The abomination, or pollution, that makes desolate' is an expression taken from Daniel (9: 27; cf. 11: 21) and presumably referred in the first place to the statue of himself, in the guise of Zeus Olympios, placed by Antiochus Epiphanes in the temple in 168 B.C. But the temple had been profaned more than once since then, e.g. by Pompey, nor need we seek for some further occasion on which a pagan statue was placed in the temple. St Luke in fact avoids this enigmatic expression, and says: 'When you shall see Jerusalem surrounded by armies.' The coming of the Romans could certainly be foreseen, but perhaps St Mark does not want to refer to them explicitly, but simply asks his readers to understand and *interpret* Daniel: so too St John in his Apocalypse refers to the Wild Beast (the enemy of God and of His Son) 'in cipher' and bids any reader of sufficient wits to decode his words. St Mark therefore foresees the advent of the Romans as the sign of the destruction of the City (cf. verse 4) and our Lord bids the inhabitants of Judea to fly while there is yet time: 'to the mountains' may be a reminiscence of 1 Macc. 2: 28; there were no mountains save far off in e.g. Moab to which a population might fly: but the expression is probably a stereotyped one. The Christians, Eusebius tells us, fled across the Jordan to Pella.

15, 16. These are vivid expressions marking the need of rapid flight.

17, 18. Women with little children, or pregnant, would naturally be in greater distress in the winter; heavy rains would swell the water-courses into torrents.

18. But pray ye that these things happen not in the winter.
19. For in those days shall be such tribulations as were not from the beginning of the creation which God created until now: neither shall be.
20. And unless the Lord had shortened the days, no flesh should be saved: but, for the sake of the elect which he hath chosen, he hath shortened the days.
21. And then if any man shall say to you: Lo, here is Christ. Lo, he is there: do not believe.
22. For there will rise up false christs and false prophets: and they shall shew signs and wonders, to seduce (if it were possible) even the elect.
23. Take you heed therefore: behold, I have foretold you all things.

---

19. Here the perspective suddenly changes just as it does in Dan. 12: 1, where after the indication that the all-conquering enemy is to become helpless (9: 45) the prophet suddenly says: 'But at that time ("at that time", "in those days", are vague expressions really meaning "any time in the future") . . . a time shall come such as never was from the time that people began to exist upon the earth up to *that* time.' (St Mark, using the very words of Daniel, writes οἷα οὐ γέγονεν τοιαύτη instead of the normal τοιαύτη . . . οἷα: this may be a unique case of such an inversion.) The phrase 'from the beginning of creation up to that time' is found elsewhere and may be part of the 'dialect' used when speaking of the 'last times'. It cannot be said that with the exception of the actual ending of human history nothing more awful than the siege and sack of Jerusalem has happened.

20–23. 'Shortened'; (ἐκολόβωσεν); literally, 'amputated': cf. Dan. 9: 24. The 'elect' signifies that those chosen from all mankind, not merely the Jews, are in question. So the allusion to 'false christs and false prophets' is no mere repetition of verse 6: these last-named are a more terrifying phenomenon: we need not suppose that they will say literally 'I am Christ' and work miracles of the sort that He did: the apparent triumph of an atheist view of life over large parts of a continent, the

The 'Eschatological Discourse' (v): 24-27

(Matt. 24: 29-31; Luke 21: 25-28)

24. But in those days, after that tribulation, the sun shall be darkened and the moon shall not give her light.

25. And the stars of heaven shall be falling down and the powers that are in heaven shall be moved.

26. And then shall they see the Son of man coming in the clouds, with great power and glory.

27. And then shall he send his angels and shall gather together his elect from the four winds, from the uttermost part of the earth to the uttermost part of heaven.

---

defection of large masses of Catholics, would be a major temptation for many.

24, 25. All these expressions are a regular part of 'apocalyptic dialect': cf. Is. 13: 10; 34: 4; Ezech. 32: 7; Joel 2: 10. They had long been purely metaphorical. Isaias uses them about the fall of Babylon and of Edom: Ezechiel, of that of Egypt. They remained in use for centuries and could be applied e.g. to the death of an important Jew. The 'powers' in the sky are the same as the stars or anything else that is supermundane (cf. Is. 34: 4). The point is, that when everything seems lost, Salvation comes.

26. Dan. 7: 13: but there the apparition means primarily 'one in human form' as contrasted with the beasts of the previous visions: our Lord has made the title 'Son of Man' so peculiarly His own, that the sentence is equivalent to: 'you shall see *me* coming . . . and I will send *my* angels'.

27. 'Winds', i.e. the four corners of the earth, conceived of as flat. Possibly the 'uttermost part of heaven' is really identical with the 'uttermost part of earth', since the sky is pictured as a vault resting on the earth. See Deut. 30: 4; Zach. 2: 6; 1 Thess. 4: 15, 16; 1 Cor. 15: 51-53.

The 'Eschatological Discourse' (vi): 28–31
(Matt. 24: 32–35; Luke 21: 29–33)

28. Now of the fig tree learn ye a parable. When the branch thereof is now tender and the leaves are come forth, you know that summer is very near.

29. So you also when you shall see these things come to pass, know ye that it is very nigh, even at the doors.

30. Amen, I say to you that this generation shall not pass until all these things be done.

31. Heaven and earth shall pass away: but my word shall not pass away.

The 'Eschatological Discourse' (vii): 32–37
(Matt. 29: 36; cf. 42; 25: 13; Luke 12: 40, and St Luke's summing-up, 20: 34–36)

32. But of that day or hour no man knoweth, neither the angels in heaven, nor the Son, but the Father.

---

28. 'From the fig tree learn what it teaches (τὴν παραβολήν)': 'tender', ἀπαλός: soft, because the sap mounts and the dried rigid wood of winter grows supple. Why should the fig tree in particular suggest the approach of summer? Because while it puts forth leaves later than the almond-blossom, biting winds (that can injure the blossom) come no more when the fig-leaves appear—they are the true sign of spring, i.e. March. Our Lord's perspective narrows again: He returns to the

30. starting-point, i.e. the sack of Jerusalem. 'This generation' must therefore be taken in its normal sense—men now living: and indeed the prophecy was fulfilled.

31. That is, 'Heaven and earth shall pass away rather than my words be unfulfilled': Matt. 5: 18 uses this expression about the permanence of the moral law: cf. Luke 16: 17.

32. 'But, as for that day or hour . . .' Our Lord returns in this verse to the End. Note that here St Mark calls our Lord, absolutely, 'the Son', as distinct from the Father, and has abandoned the term 'Son of Man'. How then can the Son of God made Man be ignorant of anything? It is held that

33. Take ye heed, watch and pray. For ye know not when the time is.

34. Even as a man who, going into a far country, left his house and gave authority to his servants over every work and commanded the porter to watch.

35. Watch ye therefore (for you know not when the lord of the house cometh, at even, or at midnight, or at the cock-crowing, or in the morning):

36. Lest coming on a sudden, he find you sleeping.

37. And what I say to you, I say to all: Watch.

---

even the Human Nature of our Lord was illuminated by His Divine Nature; and it is argued that He did not 'know' the time of the Last Coming because it was no part of His mission to reveal it. It may be asked if the End of the World *can* be stated in terms of our 'time', since, when it occurs, time in our sense will have ceased. But only in terms of our time could any answer have been intelligible to the human mind.

33. Our Lord emphatically tells them that they have received no sign of the Ending of the World or of His Second Coming. Of the End of Jerusalem, and of a whole period of human history, yes.

34–37. Another 'parable', recalling that of the talents (Matt. 25: 14 ff.; or that of the servants waiting for their master (Luke 12: 36 ff.): the servants were not given authority so much as freedom each to do his work: the mention of the 'porter' brings the parable back to its main point, i.e. watchfulness. We may hold, then, that in one and the same discourse our Lord treated of two topics—the sack of Jerusalem, preceded by recognizable 'signs'; and the Second Coming, of which there would be no signs. Flight from the approaching Romans would be possible: none could escape the Advent of the Lord: therefore—let all be on their guard, lest they be taken unawares.

CHAPTER FOURTEEN

The Plot to Arrest Our Lord: 1, 2

(Matt. 26: 1–5; Luke 22: 1–2)

1. Now the feast of the pasch and of the Azymes was after two days: and the chief priests and the scribes sought how they might by some wile lay hold on him and kill him.
2. But they said: Not on the festival day, lest there should be a tumult among the people.

---

1. For the chronology of the Passion see the note at the end of the chapter. The 'Pasch' was the feast commemorating the rescue from Egypt, and included the eating of the paschal lamb on the evening of the 14th of the month Nisan. The feast of Unleavened Bread followed the Pasch, but since Jewish feasts always began on the eve, it too began on the evening of 14th Nisan, the actual feast being celebrated on the 15th Nisan, and continued, less solemnly, for seven days. 'After two days' must here be taken literally: 'The Pasch and the Azymes were to take place "two days later"', i.e. on Thursday evening and Friday. The concern of our Lord's enemies was, then, how to get hold of Him—once they had done that, His death could easily be managed: they discussed the matter, because while some were saying: 'Not on the actual feast-day, because there would be a popular tumult': others could urge 'not afterwards; for He might easily slip out with the other Galileans: therefore there was need for haste—the arrest must take place quickly.'

A difficulty arises from St John's placing this episode six days before the Pasch, whereas in Matthew and Mark it seems clearly to be on the Wednesday, 12th Nisan. Possibly

The Anointing at Bethania: 3–9
(Matt. 27: 6–13; John 12: 1–8)

3. And when he was in Bethania, in the house of Simon the leper, and was at meat, there came a woman having an alabaster box of ointment of precious spikenard. And breaking the alabaster box, she poured it out upon his head.

4. Now there were some that had indignation within themselves and said: Why was this waste of the ointment made?

St Matthew and St Mark (St Luke omits it, maybe because he had already recorded an unction-scene (7: 36–50)) place the episode here, as accounting for the grudge felt by Judas, whom however St Mark does not name. Possibly, too, the reference to burial brought it to the minds of writers conscious of the imminence of the Passion.

3. Simon was of course cured. St John says the woman was called Mary: St Matthew and St Mark do not name her, even when saying (9) that her action would for ever be commemorated. She brought an alabaster (or onyx: *nardi . . . onyx*, cf. Horace, *Odes*, iv, 12) flask with a thin neck, such as perfumes were usually kept in: 'nard' was a species of myrrh; and 'precious' (πιστική), almost certainly means 'genuine', for Pliny tells us that this scented ointment might be adulterated: *this* ointment was pure. Only St Mark tells how she broke the neck off—thus the flask became useless: its office had been to anoint our Lord, and thereafter served no more. St John uses St Mark's description of the ointment, but says it was poured on to our Lord's feet—surely a natural act! To pour a whole flaskful over the head would have been too lavish!

4. St Mark does not say who protested: St Matthew specifies the disciples: only St John names Judas. It is useless to try to reckon what 300 denarii would amount to today, since the value of money keeps changing: a denarius was however a labourer's daily wage (Matt. 20: 2 and cf. Mark 6: 37).

5. For this ointment might have been sold for more than three hundred pence and given to the poor. And they murmured against her.

6. But Jesus said: Let her alone. Why do you molest her? She hath wrought a good work upon me.

7. For the poor you have always with you: and whensoever you will, you may do them good: but me you have not always.

8. She hath done what she could: she is come beforehand to anoint my body for the burial.

9. Amen, I say to you, wheresoever this gospel shall be preached in the whole world, that also which she hath done shall be told for a memorial of her.

The Treachery of Judas: 10, 11
(Matt. 26: 14–16; Luke 22: 3–6)

10. And Judas Iscariot, one of the twelve, went to the chief priests, to betray him to them.

11. Who hearing it were glad: and they promised him they would give him money. And he sought how he might conveniently betray him.

---

7. Our Lord is speaking to the disciples; He does not prophesy that poverty will always exist (though there are no signs of
8. its disappearing): He states the existing fact. 'She has done what she could': doubtless she herself saw no further than a mark of honour given to our Lord: but *He* sees in her act an anticipation of the anointing of His dead body, which, after all, could not be done properly on the day of his burial. Notice how our Lord foresees even the details of His history becoming everywhere known.

11. They were glad, because they had no definite plan of their own. Now they have a spontaneous offer from a companion of Jesus Himself. We cannot trace the progressive decline of Judas's faith or devotion, though see John 6: 71. He could not have started merely because he hoped our Lord would be the Messias and that he himself would gain by belonging to the Conqueror's intimate band, for, he was *called*. A modern man, who loses vocation, or faith, may try to efface himself

136

Preparation for the Pasch: 12–16

(Matt. 26: 17–19; Luke 21: 7–13)

12. Now on the first day of the unleavened bread, when they sacrificed the pasch, the disciples say to him: Whither wilt thou that we go and prepare for thee to eat the pasch?

13. And he sendeth two of his disciples and saith to them: Go ye into the city; and there shall meet you a man carrying a pitcher of water. Follow him.

---

from a religious Order, or the Church, as quietly as possible: not so an Oriental. Love turns to hate: Judas not only deserts our Lord, but goes over to the enemy. Besides, he was greedy for gain, and in Matthew we see that he *asks* for money: cf. John 12: 6: he was a 'thief', yet our Lord does not forcibly prevent him from sin or its occasion.

12. 'The first day of the unleavened bread' or 'of the Azymes' creates a difficulty in Latin. The 'Azymes', as we have said, lasted a week, beginning on the 15th Nisan. But, for a Jew, that feast began on the evening of the 14th Nisan. But the 14th Nisan was Friday, when our Lord was crucified. Now it is certain that in later Greek $\pi\rho\hat{\omega}\tau\sigma\varsigma$, the word here translated 'first', could mean $\pi\rho\acute{\sigma}\tau\epsilon\rho\sigma\varsigma$, i.e. earlier, and in short $\pi\rho\acute{\sigma}$, i.e. 'before': we would have, then, '*before* the day of the Azymes, etc.', which would bring us back to the 13th, Thursday. In Aramaic, too, there was a word meaning both 'first' and 'before'. Many of the Greek Fathers explicitly take the word in this sense. But while both Greek and Aramaic admit of this double sense, *prima dies* in Latin can mean nothing but 'the first day': hence the difficulty does not arise from what is said, but from the language in which it is said.

13. This is certainly given as a sign of our Lord's foreknowledge: even so, we must remember the dense crowds thronging the city and its surroundings: surely many would have been carrying water-jars? It has been noted that today, at any rate, women carry water in jars; men, in skins: this man would, then, have been an exception.

14. And whithersoever he shall go in, say to the master of the house, The master saith, Where is my refectory, where I may eat the pasch with my disciples?

15. And he will shew you a large dining room furnished. And there prepare ye for us.

16. And his disciples went their way and came into the city. And they found as he had told them: and they prepared the pasch.

Warning of the Betrayal: 17–21

(Matt. 26: 20–25; Luke 22: 14, 21–23; John 13: 21–30)

17. And when evening was come, he cometh with the twelve.

18. And when they were at table and eating, Jesus saith: Amen I say to you, one of you that eateth with me shall betray me.

19. But they began to be sorrowful and to say to him, one by one: Is it I?

20. Who saith to them: One of the twelve, who dippeth with me his hand in the dish.

---

14. Does '*my* dining-room' imply that the owner of the house already knew our Lord?

15. The man would show them to a large upper-storey room, ready furnished with. mats and cushions (ἐστρωμένον).

17. 'With the Twelve': evidently the two sent ahead (named Peter and John by St Luke) had returned to say that all was ready.

18. The Jews no longer ate standing, according to the earliest regulation (Ex. 7: 3–16), but lying (even the slaves) round a circular table, or in a semicircle to show they were free from foreign rule. They propped themselves on their left elbow, leaving the right hand free.

20. Our Lord leaves the answer vague (what He said to St John, 13: 23 ff., was spoken in a whisper: see on John *loc. cit.*). The 'dish' may have contained a sauce in which lettuce or herbs were dipped; or a sort of 'fruit salad' sprinkled with vinegar, into which too herbs were dipped.

21. 'Goeth': ὑπάγειν is often used by St John to indicate our

21. And the Son of man indeed goeth, as it is written of him: but woe to that man by whom the Son of man shall be betrayed. It were better for him, if that man had not been born.

The Holy Eucharist: 22–25
(Matt. 26: 26–29; Luke 22: 17–20; cf. 1 Cor. 11: 23–25)

22. And whilst they were eating, Jesus took bread; and blessing, broke and gave to them and said: Take ye. This is my body.

23. And having taken the chalice, giving thanks, he gave it to them. And they all drank of it.

Lord's dying (8: 14, 21; 13: 3, 33; 14: 4); and indicates how *freely* our Lord went to His Passion. If 'Alas for that man . . .' is a sigh rather than a 'malediction'; and even what follows is 'conditional': Judas could still have repented, and perhaps, even as he hanged himself, he did.

22. 'Bread' (ἄρτος) is normally used of leavened bread: but at the paschal supper unleavened bread was used, because it was *also* the eve of the 'Azymes'. The blessing and breaking and distribution make us look back to the miracle of the loaves and fishes (6: 41; 8: 6) save that here it is our Lord who gives to each, not the disciples who distribute. In Aramaic our Lord could have said only: 'This, my Body', so no argument can be based on the word 'is' (ἐστίν) as though it might mean 'represents'. St Paul adds: τὸ ὑπὲρ ὑμῶν: 'that is for your sakes'.

23. 'Taking a cup': in the paschal meal, wine was drunk four times; but each had his own cup. Here St Mark emphasizes that they all drank from the same cup. This is an indication that our Lord did not celebrate a *normal* Pasch, nor is there any mention of a lamb being bought or eaten, or indeed killed in the Temple as the paschal lambs would be next day. If, as we hold, this was *not* a normal ceremonial Pasch (see p. 151), we need not try to detect each of the paschal rites in what the Gospels tell us.

24. And he said to them: This is my blood of the new testament, which shall be shed for many.

25. Amen I say to you that I will drink no more of the fruit of the vine until that day when I shall drink it new in the kingdom of God.

---

24. This does not mean that our Lord pronounced these words after He had consecrated the cup and the disciples had drunk from it, for in that case they would not have known what the Cup consisted of and symbolized when they drank from it. He will have acted in regard of the Cup as He did of the Bread. 'This is my Blood of the Covenant which is being poured out for many' (omit 'new'—καινήν—probably introduced here (though not into Matthew) to harmonize with Luke and Paul). Read 'is being poured out' (ἐκχυννόμενον), not the future. The Last Supper was already a sacrificial meal: Calvary consummated it; and Mass 're-presents' it, i.e. continuously offers to God a sacrifice which is one and the same with the original one. 'Testament', or Covenant (διαθήκη), looks back to Ex. 24: 8: 'Behold the blood of the alliance that the Lord has made with you (ἰδοὺ τὸ αἷμα τῆς διαθήκης ἧς διέθετο κύριος πρὸς ὑμᾶς). But by the time of the New Testament, it seems that διαθήκη was normally if not always used in the sense of 'testament', i.e. 'will': both senses should be retained: this is that Alliance of which the former was but the foreshadowing; and, our Lord 'bequeaths' His death and redeeming blood to mankind. 'For many' does not mean 'not for all', but marks the contrast between the One who sheds His blood and the many who profit by it if they will.

25. St Luke puts these words before the Institution of the Holy Eucharist: in that case, the consecrated Cup would itself be the new wine (καινόν, not νέον: different in kind, not of 'recent vintage'). Our Lord means 'in heaven', which He symbolizes as a banquet (cf. Matt. 22: 1; Luke 14: 16): there, everything is transformed—'For the heaven shall be new, and the earth new' (Is. 65: 17, etc.; and Apoc. 21: 1:

Prophecy of Peter's Denial: 26–31

(Matt. 26: 30–35; cf. Luke 22: 31–39; John 13: 36–38; 16: 32)

26. And when they had sung an hymn, they went forth to the mount of Olives.

27. And Jesus saith to them: You will all be scandalized in my regard this night. For it is written: *I will strike the shepherd, and the sheep shall be dispersed.*

28. But after I shall be risen again, I will go before you into Galilee.

'And I saw a new heaven and a new earth', and 5: 'Behold, I make all things new').

26. If Ex. 12: 22 forbade the Hebrews to leave their house on the paschal night: 'custom' expanded 'house' to mean 'Jerusalem', and the near side of the Mount of Olives would have been regarded as within the Jerusalem area, but not Bethany on the east slope of the mountain. And if this was not the official paschal meal, the regulation would not have to be considered.

St Matthew writes as St Mark does: St Luke and St John place the prediction of Peter's denial and his protest earlier, while they are still at table. An instance of the Evangelists stating 'what matters' only. What 'mattered' was what was said, not *where*. 'Scandalized'—thrown off your balance: 'in my regard' is an addition. The prophecy (Zach. 13: 7) was: 'Sword, . . . strike the shepherd, and the flock shall be scattered.' Again, our Lord *refers* to the Scripture rather than quotes it verbatim.

28. As usual, the serene assertion of the resurrection follows that of the Passion. It seems as if our Lord had meant the apostles to go straight to Galilee—yet He would be there before them! But even after the resurrection, they were still so bewildered and almost stunned by the succession of events, that they

29. stayed a week or more in Jerusalem. Peter's cry was that of wounded affection, not of vain self-sufficiency in comparison with the others.

29. But Peter saith to him: Although all shall be scandalized in thee, yet not I.

30. And Jesus saith to him: Amen I say to thee, to day, even in this night, before the cock crow twice, thou shalt deny me thrice.

31. But he spoke the more vehemently: Although I should die together with thee, I will not deny thee. And in like manner also said they all.

The Agony in the Garden: 32-42

(Matt. 26: 36-46; Luke 22: 40-46. Cf. John 18: 1 ff.)

32. And they came to a farm called Gethsemani. And he saith to his disciples: Sit you here, while I pray.

33. And he taketh Peter and James and John with him: and he began to fear and to be heavy.

34. And he saith to them: My soul is sorrowful even unto death. Stay you here and watch.

---

30. Every word is emphatic: 'I say to you that *you*—today—this very night . . .' To 'deny' was much stronger than to 'be scandalized'. Cock-crow in March–April could be very early, e.g. 3 a.m. And several cock-crows could follow one another rapidly. Matthew and Mark are here fuller than Luke and John.

32. 'Farm' ($\chi\acute{\omega}\rho\iota o\nu$): a small estate: even (as in John) a garden. The name means an 'oil-press': it was across the rivulet Kedron and at the foot of the hill. It was, very early, a place of pilgrimage: special ceremonies took place there in Holy Week: the apse of a church had been found precisely within the enclosure and it has been rebuilt. St Matthew tells that our Lord pointed out where He was going—'yonder'. St Luke ever since the beginning of the Last Supper clearly follows a different tradition from St Mark's.

33. 'Fear' ($\dot{\epsilon}\kappa\theta\alpha\mu\beta\epsilon\hat{\iota}\sigma\theta\alpha\iota$): 'out of himself with appalment': 'heavy', ($\dot{\alpha}\delta\eta\mu o\nu\epsilon\hat{\iota}\nu$) is a rare word, and joined by Plato with $\dot{\alpha}\pi o\rho\epsilon\hat{\iota}\nu$: He was 'at a loss', aghast.

34. $\Pi\epsilon\rho\acute{\iota}\lambda\upsilon\pi o\varsigma$: 'in utter anguish' rather than 'sorrowful': so much so that He felt He could have died of it (cf. Jonas 4:

35. And when he was gone forward a little, he fell flat on the ground: and he prayed that, if it might be, the hour might pass from him.

36. And he saith: Abba, Father, all things are possible to thee: remove this chalice from me; but not what I will, but what thou wilt.

37. And he cometh and findeth them sleeping. And he saith to Peter: Simon, sleepest thou? Couldst thou not watch one hour?

9: σφόδρα λελύπημαι ἐγὼ ἕως θανάτου). The immediate cause of this distress was His vivid realization of all that His imminent Passion meant. Devout writers see the cause of it in His divine perception that His sacrifice would be in vain for so many. That was perhaps included; but we must not risk losing sight of the reality of what our Lord, in His human nature, endured.

35. 'He fell', (ἔπιπτεν): imperfect. He kept falling prostrate, rising, and falling again: Orientals are not reticent after our fashion; no doubt our Lord's cries could be heard at first by the apostles: He had gone ahead, says St Mark, μικρόν, only 'a little'. It was wholly right that every nerve in our Lord's body, and every human thought in His mind, should shrink with horror and indignation from the torments, injustice, treachery and lies to which He was about to fall victim. He does not hesitate to express this, but also His complete self-abandonment to God's will, and the full free submission of His own. These interior states of shrinking and acceptance can *exist* together, but they cannot be simultaneously *expressed* in outward words.

37. 'Sleep' is often the reaction from an extreme nervous and emotional strain: 'Simon' is a mark of affection rather than a comment or a rebuke due to the apostle's being so un-Rocklike. 'The spirit indeed . . .' Our Lord even makes this gentle excuse. 'An hour' (ὥρα) here means a short while, not a clock-hour: they had not been 'strong enough' even for that: in 35, the 'hour' means the terrible time of doom as often in John, and is really the same as the 'cup' (10: 38).

38. Watch ye: and pray that you enter not into temptation. The spirit indeed is willing, but the flesh is weak.

39. And going away again, he prayed, saying the same words.

40. And when he returned, he found them again asleep (for their eyes were heavy): and they knew not what to answer him.

41. And he cometh the third time and saith to them: Sleep ye now and take your rest. It is enough. The hour is come: behold the Son of man shall be betrayed into the hands of sinners.

42. Rise up: let us go. Behold, he that will betray me is at hand.

The Arrest: 43–50
(Matt. 26: 47–56; Luke 22: 47–53; John 18: 2–12)

43. And while he was yet speaking, cometh Judas Iscariot, one of the twelve: and with him a great multitude with swords and staves, from the chief priests and the scribes and the ancients.

44. And he that betrayed him had given them a sign, saying: Whomsoever I shall kiss, that is he. Lay hold on him: and lead him away carefully.

---

38. 'Enter into temptation': they must not merely pray not to be tempted: temptation is always at hand, like a net or snare: they must pray lest they walk into it: our Lord prayed: the disciples slept.

40. They were still stupefied with sleep; they had no words to say to Him.

41. Our Lord in His humanity needed companionship, and in great anguish men are often restless: but when He came for the third time, He said with grave irony: 'Sleep on, now, and take your rest!' But no—'Enough of this', $\dot{a}\pi\acute{e}\chi\epsilon\iota$: Prayer, sleep . . . all that is now over: 'The hour has struck': 'Up! let us go. He who is betraying me is at hand!'

43. 'Multitude', $\ddot{o}\chi\lambda o\varsigma$: a 'crowd', not a regular band of soldiers or temple-servants, though some of these may well have been there too: also, some individual members of the three groups composing the Sanhedrin: even today, or quite recently,

45. And when he was come, immediately going up to him, he saith: Hail, Rabbi! And he kissed him.

46. But they laid hands on him and held him.

47. And one of them that stood by, drawing a sword, struck a servant of the chief priest and cut off his ear.

48. And Jesus answering, said to them: Are you come out as to a robber, with swords and staves to apprehend me?

49. I was daily with you in the temple teaching: and you did not lay hands on me. But that the scriptures may be fulfilled.

50. Then his disciples, leaving him, all fled away.

---

shepherds round Jerusalem carry a 'cutlass' in their girdle and hold a club.

44. 'A sign' ($\sigma\acute{v}\sigma\sigma\eta\mu o\nu$), a *tessera*; a sign agreed upon. Only St Mark adds: 'Seize him, and take him off safely'.

45. 'When he was come, immediately going up to him', $\acute{\epsilon}\lambda\theta\grave{\omega}\nu$ $\pi\rho o\sigma\epsilon\lambda\theta\acute{\omega}\nu$ is unusual but vivid: Judas came right up to Him: 'kissed'; $\kappa\alpha\tau\epsilon\phi\acute{\iota}\lambda\eta\sigma\epsilon\nu$: almost 'hugged': he clung to Him till all could be sure it was He.

47. 'One of them', ($\epsilon\emph{i}s$ $\tau\iota s$): 'a certain one of those present'; in John we see it was Peter. Why did he not allow himself to be named here, because the act, though in a sense courageous, was not really to his credit? Perhaps he still felt that in a sense it *was*—'I was the only one who made *some* resistance!'

48, 49. Our Lord seems to resent the indignity of this arrest: it was indecent to treat Him like a brigand! 'Daily' ($\kappa\alpha\theta'$ $\acute{\eta}\mu\acute{\epsilon}\rho\alpha\nu$) need not mean more than 'often': and 'among *you*' might be inappropriate to this rabble who would hardly have been listening to our Lord: Our Lord looks beyond them to the instigators of the arrest, and indeed some of them as we said, may well have been present. The unfinished sentence: 'But that the Scriptures may be fulfilled' . . . is not only vivid but in St Mark's style.

The Young Man in a Linen Cloth: 51, 52

51. And a certain young man followed him, having a linen cloth cast about his naked body. And they laid hold on him.

52. But he, casting off the linen cloth, fled from them naked.

Jesus before Caiaphas (i): 53–65
(Matt. 26: 57–68; Luke 22: 54a, 63–71; cf. John 18: 12–14; 19–24)

53. And they brought Jesus to the high priest. And all the priests and the scribes and the ancients assembled together.

51, 52. The 'linen cloth', σινδών, was a long cloth usually of fine linen: men wrapped themselves up in this when they went to bed. It is out of the question that anyone could have come from the city thus attired; we may presume that the youth came from a close-by house (perhaps the keeper's of the 'garden') having heard the noise, went out, and began to follow along with the crowd (συνηκολούθει) out of curiosity rather than sympathy: when he was noticed, it was clear he had not come with the traitor's group, so they caught hold of him: rather than get into trouble, he slipped out of the loose covering and ran away. There is no reason to suppose this was St Mark himself, though either he alone was informed of the incident or St Matthew and St Luke thought it too trivial to mention. At least it shows how completely friendless our Lord now was.

53. Neither St Mark nor St Luke names the 'high-priest'; but St Matthew and St John call him Caiaphas who in fact held that office from A.D. 18 to 36. Theoretically the high-priest-hood was a life office; but the Romans might depose any high-priest they did not like, and there were endless intrigues. Annas had been a 'political' priest and was deposed in A.D. 15. Yet five of his sons became high-priests. Caiaphas was his son-in-law. If then our Lord was first taken before Annas, it was a kind of 'visit of courtesy' to the aged 'high-priest' though he was but technically so (see John 18: 13). It is clear

54. And Peter followed him afar off, even into the court of the high priest. And he sat with the servants at the fire and warmed himself.

55. And the chief priests and all the council sought for evidence against Jesus, that they might put him to death: and found none.

56. For many bore false witness against him: and their evidences were not agreeing.

57. And some rising up, bore false witness against him, saying:

58. We heard him say, I will destroy this temple made with hands, and within three days I will build another not made with hands.

---

that the actual interrogations took place before Caiaphas who may have lived in the same house as Annas or in one adjoining it and separated only by the open 'court', perhaps where

54. Peter sat among the servants 'by the blaze' ($\phi\hat{\omega}\varsigma$); the fire will have been made of wood and brushwood.

55. St Mark insists again on the presence of at least some of all constituent members of the Sanhedrin. At night the Temple was closed, else they would have met in a room used for such reunions, within the temple precincts.

The Jews had no right to execute a criminal, but only to try him, decide if he were worthy of death, and then take him to the Roman procurator who alone could pronounce the final verdict. St Mark condenses the whole story: the 'Sanhedrists' had evidently expected that our Lord would say something 'blasphemous' so that they could condemn Him 'out of hand': but He did not. Therefore these unscrupulous men who were also meticulous 'legalists', had unexpectedly to hunt for at least two witnesses (Numbers 35: 30; Deut. 17: 15)—in the middle of the night, in a town asleep and packed with pilgrims. We think that it was during this time that our Lord was removed to some other room and brutally treated by His guards.

57. We further think that even if some sort of witnesses had been obtained at the first session (what they said did not sufficiently coincide), two witnesses did arrive very early and said, more or less, what is recorded in verse 58: but even so, they were

59. And their witness did not agree.
60. And the high priest rising up in the midst, asked Jesus, saying: Answerest thou nothing to the things that are laid to thy charge by these men?
61. But he held his peace and answered nothing. Again the high priest asked him and said to him: Art thou the Christ, the Son of the Blessed God?
62. And Jesus said to him: I am. And you shall see the Son of man sitting on the right hand of the power of God and coming with the clouds of heaven.
63. Then the high priest rending his garments, saith: What need we any further witnesses?
64. You have heard the blasphemy. What think you? Who all condemned him to be guilty of death.

not in exact agreement. St Matthew simply reports them as saying: 'I can destroy the temple of God and build it in three days'. St Luke omits the 'witness', which can hardly be but a reminiscence of John 2: 19: 'Destroy this temple, and in three days I will build it up', especially if, as we hold, the original words were spoken on the previous Monday.

60–64. Caiaphas cannot make adequate use of such unsatisfactory witnesses, but tries to get our Lord to speak—there are probably here two questions: 'Do you not answer anything' What is the witness that these men bear against you?? Exasperated by our Lord's silence, Caiaphas asks Him point-blank: 'Art thou the Christ, the Son of the Blessed One?' Luke's fuller account may follow the event more closely. This high-priest asks if Jesus is the Christ. He agreed, and added that He would be exalted to the right hand of God in glory. But even so, there was not yet explicit 'blasphemy', for the Jews expected the Messias to be a *man* among men. They then ask if He claimed to be Son of God—evidently in a superhuman sense, in fact, 'divine'. When He said Yes: they had the 'blasphemy' they wanted and could dispense with witnesses. But Mark is nearer rabbinic phraseology: Jews

65. And some began to spit on him and to cover his face and to buffet him and to say unto him: Prophesy. And the servants struck him with the palms of their hands.

Peter's Denials: 66–72

(Matt. 26: 69–75; Luke 22: 56–62. Cf. John 18: 17; 25–27)

66. Now when Peter was in the court below, there cometh one of the maidservants of the high priest.

---

avoided the Name of God: the high-priest speaks of 'the Son of the Blessed One': our Lord says He will be seen at the right of 'the Power' ('of God' is an addition). The result is the same: the high-priest had authority to ask: our Lord could not any more refrain from acknowledging the truth about Himself. His words look back to Dan. 7: 9, 13, but add to it. Daniel had spoken of 'thrones' and of the approach of a figure in human form: our Lord says that *He* is the Son of Man, and is to sit upon the throne at God's right hand—in the same 'rank' as God. When a blasphemy was heard (or even repeated by a witness), a judge was bound to tear his clothes—but 'custom' had stereotyped the place and size of the rent: it had become a technicality—an inch or so, at the neck.

65. No doubt even as our Lord was taken from the assembly, some of the Sanhedrists spat at Him—a common display of disgust among the Jews (Deut. 25: 9; Job 30: 10, etc.: predicted by our Lord, 10: 34): they blindfolded Him and hit Him: 'buffet', κολαφίζειν, can mean to hit with the fist or the back of the hand: 'struck': (ῥάπισμα, below, means rather, to strike with the flat of the hand): 'Prophesy' means: 'Tell us who hit you!' So Matthew and Luke explicitly.

66. St Mark goes back to an earlier hour. Our Lord had been taken to a higher room: Peter and the guard and servants remained in the open court. 'A maid-servant': (παιδίσκη), a young slave-girl.

67. And when she had seen Peter warming himself, looking on him, she saith: Thou also wast with Jesus of Nazareth.

68. But he denied, saying: I neither know nor understand what thou sayest. And he went forth before the court: and the cock crew.

69. And again a maidservant seeing him, began to say to the standers by: This is one of them.

70. But he denied again. And after a while they that stood by said again to Peter: Surely thou art one of them; for thou art also a Galilean.

71. But he began to curse and to swear, saying: I know not this man of whom you speak.

---

67. She 'saw' Peter and 'stared' at him. Her words are in an unusual order: 'You too were with the Nazarene—Jesus!'

68. 'I don't know . . . I don't understand what you mean.' Not 'I don't know *Him*.' He went out of the court, but no further than the forecourt or vestibule, where it was darker. Several MSS. omit the cock-crow (30 and 72 make it clear that it occurred): Peter's distressed mind may easily not have 'registered' it.

69. St Mark certainly suggests that this was the same servant, and that she renewed her 'attack': But St Matthew says 'another maid': and St Luke alludes to 'men' as occasioning the second and third denial. This is an example of the way in which the evangelists composed their documents. There was a central fact—the triple denial. This is their point and on it they coincide. As to what led up to the denials, tradition was uncertain and each evangelist followed the best that he knew. We presume that St Mark was the most accurate, for St Peter will surely have remembered the circumstances of his great tragedy.

70. All the company is now alert and joins in the attack, noticing too that his accent was Galilean. It is said that this sounded so boorish to the Jews that they would not allow Galileans to read in their synagogues. Probably Peter had been hustled back into the main court, especially as St Luke (22: 61) says

72. And immediately the cock crew again. And Peter remembered the word that Jesus had said unto him: Before the cock crow twice, thou shalt thrice deny me. And he began to weep.

---

that our Lord turned (as He was being led out?) and looked at Peter.

71. Strictly speaking, 'to curse and to swear' should mean to call God to witness, and to invoke curses on oneself should one be speaking falsely.

72. The second cock-crow reaches Peter's consciousness: he went out and (ἔκλαιεν) began to weep. But this avoids the difficult Greek word ἐπιβαλών. This could mean: 'covering his head', or 'reflecting'—putting his mind to it, but more probably marks the intensity of his distress: St Matthew and St Luke say that he wept *bitterly*, thus avoiding the obscure word. A papyrus has a parallel—'set to, and wept' would be a literal translation: the sense is: 'He burst into tears and went on weeping'.

Note on the Nature of the Last Supper

The difficulty is this—all are agreed that our Lord was crucified on a Friday. St John makes it clear that the 'Paschal Meal' was eaten by our Lord's enemies that night: the Synoptists seem to state that it was eaten on the previous night. What was this meal? In Exodus 12 we read that on the 10th day of the first month (afterwards called Nisan) a lamb must be chosen and kept till the 14th when it would be sacrificed in the evening and eaten that night, roasted, with unleavened bread and bitter herbs; it was to be eaten hastily, clothes girt up, sandals on feet, staff in hand—for the Israelites were on the point of leaving Egypt. 'This is the Pasch, or Passover, of Yahweh.' This was followed by the ceremony of 'unleavened bread' which lasted for seven days, during which leaven was forbidden. But since Jewish celebrations (and indeed any 'day') were calculated from the previous nightfall (compare our 'Eves'), leaven had to be got rid of on the evening of the Pasch. The two events overlapped. In our Lord's time the paschal ceremony was, briefly, as follows—the master of the house took a cup of wine, the first of four (each participant had his own) and blessed it. Then bitter herbs were dipped in a kind of sauce, the Charoseth, and distributed. Then the origin of this ritual was explained, part of the 'Hallel' (Ps. 114–117) was sung and a second cup was drunk. Then cakes of unleavened bread were broken, blessed and distributed: the Paschal Lamb was eaten. Then a third cup, 'the Cup of Blessing', was blessed and drunk: the rest of those psalms were sung and the fourth cup drunk. The 'standing up', etc., symbolizing the flight from Egypt, was given up, the Jews being now free and not needing to escape from slavery. In our Lord's time, then, the lamb had to be bought and killed in the Temple on the afternoon of the 'Preparation' of the Pasch, 14th Nisan, and eaten that night which counted already as the beginning of the Feast, 15th Nisan. Now St John makes it indisputable that our Lord died on the day of the Preparation of the Pasch, which was therefore kept on Saturday (Sabbath) that year, which is why he emphasizes that it was a 'great' sabbath-day. The Jews would not enter the (pagan) Pilate's hall lest they should incur a ceremonial taint and so be unable to eat the Pasch (which therefore they had not yet eaten: 18: 28). In 19: 14 St John says definitely that it was the Preparation of the Pasch (perhaps too in 19: 31). When Judas leaves the supper-room, the disciples think he may be going to buy what would be needed for the Feast. But if the Thursday was the Pasch itself, its evening was also the beginning of the sacred 'week' of unleavened bread, and its first day was one on which no work could be done so that neither could Judas have bought anything nor all the arrangements for the arrest and trial of Jesus have been carried through—Herod Agrippa who did arrest Peter during that week could not proceed to his execution (which he intended) while the week was still unfinished (Acts 12: 3 ff.). We may even notice that the Synoptists themselves apparently do not regard the Friday as the Paschal day itself (when no work could be done) since not only the Cyrenaean returns from the country, possibly from field-work there (Mark 15: 21 and parallels): but a winding-sheet can be bought (Mark 15: 46) and also spices (Luke 23: 56), and the police and even Peter carry weapons (Mark 14: 47).

However, the Synoptists certainly seem to mean that our Lord *did* eat *a* 'Paschal' meal with His disciples: He made them make preparations for such a meal (Mark 14: 12 ff.; Matt. 26: 17; Luke 22: 7): and the following verses state that these preparations were carried out—save that no mention is here or later made of a *lamb*, which could be obtained only next afternoon, and in fact only if it had been killed in the Temple precincts: indeed, Josephus says that (in A.D. 65) 256,500 lambs were thus killed between three and five o'clock —basing himself on the reckoning that about three million Jews were then in or around Jerusalem. This may be exaggerated; anyhow the normal hour for sacrifice—three to three-thirty—had to be prolonged to allow for this immense lamb-massacre. It remains that St Luke (22: 15 ff.) explicitly says that our Lord earnestly wished to eat '*this* Pasch together with you'. Yet, if one had only the scriptural accounts of the meal to read, no one would have thought it was a paschal meal. No mention of the lamb: or of the bitter herbs: or of the fourfold drinking, by each, of a cup, or of any allusion to the first Passover when the Israelites escaped from Egypt; no definite reference to the 'Hallel'. We do not think that any theory about e.g. Galileans having calculated their week differently from the Judeans or the permission to celebrate the Pasch a day earlier, or later, than the official one, can be maintained. An opinion, held by many, is that our Lord did *not* celebrate the official Pasch, but '*His*' Pasch, the only Pasch that henceforward would matter. St Paul said: 'Christ our Pasch, is sacrificed for us' (1 Cor. 5: 17). We think, then, that on the day of the Last Supper, the Apostles may

well at first have been bewildered by what was happening—
for our Lord seemed to speak of it as a 'Pasch', and yet it was
the wrong day for that—but that as the evening proceeded
they realized that He was inaugurating something new—a
new Alliance; a new Bequest—and have known that when
they received the mysterious Bread and Wine it was Himself
with whom they were being intimately united. The notion
of the New Pasch gradually so completely superseded an
affair of ritual days and hours that they felt and spoke of the
Last Supper as *His* 'Pasch'; *He* the Lamb; theirs the true
Exodus. As if, *after* the Crucifixion, they would have gone
and bought a paschal lamb!

It would probably be confusing to catalogue the arguments
contrary to the above opinion. They are based largely on the
existence of two different calendars, and on the frequent
clashes between Sadducees and Pharisees on ritual matters.
But, on the balance, we think that 'the Lord of the Sabbath'
could disregard any question of dates and be concerned only
with the institution of '*His*' Pasch, *His* altogether New
Alliance, and that the Apostles gradually realized that *that* was
what was happening.

CHAPTER FIFTEEN

Jesus taken to Pilate: 1
(Matt. 27: 1–2; cf. Luke 22: 66; 23: 1; John 18: 28)

1. And straightway in the morning, the chief priests holding a consultation with the ancients and the scribes and the whole council, binding Jesus, led him away and delivered him to Pilate.

Pilate interrogates Jesus, scourges Him and gives Him up to be Crucified: 2–15
(Matt. 27: 11–26; Luke 23: 2–5; 18–25; cf. John 18: 29–40; 19: 4–16)

2. And Pilate asked him: Art thou the king of the Jews? But he answering, saith to him: Thou sayest it.

---

1. It was after 'second cock-crow' and in April; therefore about five a.m. The 'consultation' was to decide in what form precisely they should make their representations to Pilate. Pilate was procurator of Judea A.D. 26–36. He was technically dependent on the propraetor of Syria who ultimately sent him to Rome as being denounced by the Jews—why exactly, is not known. The Jew Philo quotes a letter of Agrippa I, accusing Pilate of every imaginable crime: but what we know of him suggests rather that he was a true Roman, anxious to act justly, but exasperated by the Jews, so 'uncivilized' in his eyes. At Jerusalem he may have lived, like his predecessor Florus, in the palace of the Herods on the west of the city: but probably during great feasts like the Pasch, when the place seethed with nationalist pilgrims, he quartered himself in the building called Antonia, overlooking the Temple.

2. Pilate had already been 'informed' by the priests that our Lord was a rebel (Luke 23: 2): they knew well that Pilate would

155

3. And the chief priests accused him in many things.

4. And Pilate again asked him, saying: Answerest thou nothing? Behold in how many things they accuse thee.

5. But Jesus still answered nothing: so that Pilate wondered.

6. Now on the festival day he was wont to release unto them one of the prisoners, whomsoever they demanded.

7. And there was one called Barabbas, who was put in prison with some seditious men, who in the sedition had committed murder.

---

not listen to any accusation connected with a mere Jewish superstition (as he would have regarded a charge of blasphemy), and therefore had to invent a political charge. Hence his contemptuous question. 'Thou sayest it' ($\sigma\grave{v}$ $\lambda\acute{\epsilon}\gamma\epsilon\iota\varsigma$): Emphasis is not on the pronoun: '*You* say so!', but the expression is a rather vague affirmative: our Lord never called Himself 'King of the Jews', nor was the Messias a national king in the sense in which Pilate would have taken the title. When 'many' further accusations were hurled at him, and he asked our Lord if He had nothing to say to any of it,

5. our Lord 'no longer' made a reply: the version 'still answered nothing' makes no sense, because He *had* made a previous answer. Pilate is astonished, puzzled, both by our Lord's silence, and by the unexpected zeal for the Empire shown by the Jews.

6. 'On the festival day', $\kappa\alpha\tau\grave{\alpha}$ $\acute{\epsilon}o\rho\tau\acute{\eta}v$, without an article, should mean 'on the occasion of a feast': but the freeing of a prisoner can hardly have taken place several times a year: there are classical examples of the liberation of prisoners on certain feast-days; but a papyrus of about A.D. 86 offers an almost exact parallel: the prefect of Egypt says to a prisoner: 'You deserve to be scourged, but I make a present of you ($\chi\alpha\rho\acute{\iota}\zeta\omicron\mu\alpha\acute{\iota}$ $\sigma\epsilon$) to the mob ($\tau o\hat{\iota}\varsigma$ $\acute{o}\chi\lambda o\iota\varsigma$)'; they were on the prisoner's side.

7. Apparently Barabbas was 'under arrest' but had not yet been condemned—nor, so far, had our Lord. This would have been an 'abolitio' which Roman lawyers say might be

8. And when the multitude was come up, they began to desire that he would do as he had ever done unto them.

9. And Pilate answered them and said: Will you that I release to you the king of the Jews?

10. For he knew that the chief priests had delivered him up out of envy.

11. But the chief priests moved the people, that he should rather release Barabbas to them.

12. And Pilate again answering, saith to them: What will you then that I do to the king of the Jews?

13. But they again cried out: Crucify him.

---

granted '*ob diem insignem . . . ob laetitiam aliquam*' and so forth Proconsuls had wider powers, and could free prisoners who *had* been condemned: the remission was always supposed to be granted by the Emperor himself. Bar-Abba(s) means 'Son of the Father', not unparalleled as an individual name. St Mark is not interested to tell us what or when the riot was.

8. By now the general crowd had 'come up' (ἀναβάς) from the lower town, but it is unlikely that they forced their way into the court where Pilate was seated: still, their howls could be easily heard. It is not clear exactly why they came— whether they wanted the customary release of *a* prisoner, or of Barabbas in particular, or whether they were incited to do so by those hostile to our Lord.

9. Pilate offered them Jesus (obviously less politically dangerous than Barabbas) but spoilt his offer by sneeringly calling Him 'king of the Jews': he realized that the priests were jealous of our Lord's influence and could not resist his jibe. The result was inevitable. They egged the people on to demand Barabbas.

12. Pilate asked what they wish to be done to Him whom *they called* (ὃν λέγετε: this is in the Greek, omitted in the vulgate) King of the Jews.

13. They cried out: 'Crucify him!' This was a Roman punishment, and had often been inflicted on Jews: but it was new that Jews should *ask* for its infliction on a compatriot.

14. And Pilate saith to them: Why, what evil hath he done? But they cried out the more: Crucify him.

15. And so Pilate being willing to satisfy the people, released to them Barabbas: and delivered up Jesus, when he had scourged him, to be crucified.

The Crowning with Thorns: 16–19
(Matt. 27: 27–31a; cf. John 19: 2, 3)

16. And the soldiers led him away into the court of the palace: and they called together the whole band.

---

14. Pilate, it is clear, especially from John, wished to liberate
15. Jesus, but decided to satisfy the mob (τὸ ἱκανὸν ποιῆσαι is a latinism, *satis-facere*, but had been acclimatized in Greek for some time), handed Barabbas over to them and gave Jesus over to His death. If it seems hardly credible that the enthusiasm of Palm Sunday should thus have swung to the opposite extreme, we may recall not only the fickleness of popular emotion (the 'psychology of the crowd' is an unpredictable quantity) but also that relatively few may have observed the Entry of our Lord into the City, and it is not probable that the *mass* of the Jews were now present demanding our Lord's death. Φραγελλοῦν: for the Latin *flagellare*: only in Mark and Matthew and later writers. The normal Greek word was μαστιγοῦν. The *flagellum* was composed of thongs. The kind used for slaves (*flagrum*), in grave cases, was of thongs into which knuckle-bones or the like were threaded; or else of iron chains ending in metal knobs. In either case the effects were dreadful: *secare*, *scindere* are words used of the *flagellum*: *rumpere*, *fodere* or *forare* of the *flagrum*. Roman citizens were exempt from scourging; but in the provinces scourging of non-citizens was usual before crucifixion. The victim was bound face to a post, or stooping over it.

16. The Greek has: 'into the court, that is, the praetorium'. And the soldiers are said to have been a σπεῖρα, or cohort,

17. And they clothe him with purple: and, platting a crown of thorns, they put it upon him.
18. And they began to salute him: Hail, king of the Jews.
19. And they struck his head with a reed: and they did spit on him. And bowing their knees, they adored him.

---

the normal garrison at Jerusalem. A cohort consisted of 600–500 men under a tribune (Acts 21: 31): Pilate may have brought more men from his habitual residence at Caesarea, and his own bodyguard. The barracks were in the Antonia tower. The 'praetorium' meant, in practice, the place where the commander-in-chief lodged, whether in a camp or in a town. A regular praetorium would have three courts; but wherever the Procurator placed his standards and tribunal would thereby become a 'praetorium'. The soldiers to whom our Lord was committed would have called to their comrades, but it was no official summons and we cannot suppose that hundreds of them were present. The mockery that followed was doubly bitter—first, the Romans, even though masters of the world, did not use purple cloaks or crowns (1 Macc. 7: 14) and would have been contemptuous when a Syrian king, Alexander, sent a crown and a purple robe to the Asmonaean Jonathan (ib., 10: 20); and, to dress up our Lord, still bleeding from the scourge, as a mock king was a personal affront. The wreath, or 'crown', was made of thorns, but we cannot tell to what plant they belonged. The red cloak will have been a military *chlamys*: they 'kept striking' His head with a cane that they had first placed in His hand as a sceptre: they 'kept spitting at Him' and genuflecting and derisively doing homage to Him. Ignominy and derision are the key-notes of this episode, rather than physical pain. During certain pagan feasts, a criminal condemned to death was given full license to do as he liked for some days during which he was dressed up as a king: and Philo (c. 40) relates that when king Agrippa passed through Alexandria, the Egyptians to show their scorn for him

The Way of the Cross: Simon from Cyrene: 20–22

(Matt. 27: 31b–33; Luke 22: 26–33a; John 19: 16 ff.)

20. And after they had mocked him, they took off the purple from him and put his own garments on him: and they led him out to crucify him.

---

dressed up a poor idiot almost exactly as our Lord was, only he was not maltreated or insulted but was shown mock respect. Our Lord's treatment, however, has no connection with any such thing, though soldiers during the army-Saturnalia actually killed the one who had been chosen 'king': so the whole idea of mocking a criminal about to be executed can well have been familiar to these men, and the proceeding is in keeping with the brutality of the low-caste pagan soldiery. Finally they clothed our Lord in His own garments: it is thought by some that He still wore the wreath, but the oldest paintings of the crucifixion do not show it.

The 'cross' (*patibulum*) began, as a punishment, in the East: it was used by exception in the Greek world, but constantly among the Romans. It was not at first a cross, but a stake planted in the ground, to which men could be bound for scourging, or head downwards; or the stake might be thrust upwards into their body. 'I see crosses not only of one sort, but made differently by different men' (Seneca, *Dial.* 6: 20, 3): or a 'cross' might be shaped like a Y, the victim's neck being stuck into the opening of the Y (this was called *furca*): finally we have the cross as we know it, with a transverse beam, either at the top, forming the letter T; or, allowing part of the upright to project (it may have been to this that the title over the cross was fixed). There was also a piece of wood on which the sufferer could sit (the mock crucifix on the Palatine suggests it was under the feet); probably the body had also to be roped to the cross, else its weight would have torn the hands away from the nails. St Irenaeus (*Contra Haereses*, II, 24, 4: about 190) says that a cross had *five* 'ends'

26. And the inscription of his cause was written over: THE KING OF THE JEWS.

---

in 9: 9 our Lord says explicitly: 'Are there not twelve hours in the day?' In 1: 39, we hear of the 10th; in 4: 52, of the 7th. Now quite apart from the difficulty of knowing the exact time, when clocks or watches were not available, an 'hour' did not stand for a fixed length of time as it does with us, but in the winter, when sunrise was late and sunset early, the twelve hours of day would have been less than one of our own hours, and those of the night, longer. But in April, about the equinox, the hours of day and night would have been fairly equal. So St John's 'about the sixth hour' may mean what we should call 'towards the latter part of the morning'. Now St Luke (23: 44) says that the miraculous darkness fell 'about' (ὡσεί) the 6th hour; but by then he has related many things that happened when our Lord was already on the cross. St Mark, as we saw, says that He was crucified at the 3rd hour, and (here St Luke coincides with him) that the darkness fell at the 6th hour and lasted till noon. Clearly, therefore, St Mark and St Luke are not using the same division of the day as St John's. They seem to have divided the day into 'hours' each consisting of three of our or of St John's hours—the morning, the 3rd, 6th and 9th hours. St Mark's 3rd hour, then, will contain any time from 9 to 12 o'clock. Thus if St Mark means 'after 9 but before 12', and St John, 'round about 12', their vague 'hours' may be considered sufficiently to coincide. See Ramsay, in Hasting's *Dictionary of the Bible*, supplementary vol., pp. 475 to 479, for perhaps the best discussion of Hebrew 'hours'.

26. This was the normal procedure. Dion Cassius relates that in the year A.D. 22 a man was led through the middle of the market place with the inscription declaring the reason (αἰτία) for his execution, after which he was crucified. A comparison with the wording of the 'title' in Matthew,

27. And with him they crucify two thieves: the one on his right hand, and the other on his left.

28. And the scripture was fulfilled, which saith: *And with the wicked he was reputed.*

29. And they that passed by blasphemed him, wagging their heads and saying: Vah, thou that destroyest the temple of God and in three days buildest it up again:

30. Save thyself, coming down from the cross.

31. In like manner also the chief priests, mocking, said with the scribes one to another: He saved others; himself he cannot save.

32. Let Christ the king of Israel come down now from the cross, that we may see and believe. And they that were crucified with him reviled him.

The Death of our Lord: 33–37
(Matt. 27: 45–50; Luke 23: 44–45a, 46; John 19: 28–30)

33. And when the sixth hour was come, there was darkness over the whole earth until the ninth hour.

Luke and John shows how St Mark is abbreviating his account of the Passion.

27. The two men crucified on either side of our Lord were 'brigands', not 'thieves' — highwaymen: $\lambda\eta\sigma\tau\alpha\iota$ (not $\kappa\lambda\epsilon\pi\tau\alpha\iota$) is the word used. But their infamy as it were fell back upon Jesus too.

28. This may be an addition, echoing Is. 53: 12, though St Peter, in his preaching, liked to refer to Is. 53.

29. This recalls Jeremias's Lamentations (2: 15): Cicero tells how men were crucified by the roadside: thus people coming into and out from a town would be duly terrorized.

31. These important persons did not mix with the crowd but jeered among themselves at our Lord's apparent helplessness: but even so they acknowledged that He *had* worked 'mighty works' that saved others in their distress.

33. The sixth hour was noon. The darkness was not due to a solar eclipse, impossible at full-moon-time. Nor are we to

34. And at the ninth hour, Jesus cried out with a loud voice, saying, Eloi, Eloi, lamma sabacthani? Which is, being interpreted: My God, My God, Why hast thou forsaken me?

35. And some of the standers by hearing, said: Behold he calleth Elias.

36. And one running and filling a sponge with vinegar and putting it upon a reed, gave him to drink, saying: Stay, let us see if Elias come to take him down.

---

ask how far the darkness extended—presumably it affected all who were aware of the crucifixion. In the Old Testament, not only the plague of Egypt (Ex. 10: 21 ff.) is recalled, but many prophecies which show darkness accompanying the judgment of God: Amos 8: 9; Joel 2: 10; 3: 4, 13; Is. 13: 10; Jer. 15: 9; and often.

34. These words, forming the first verse of Ps. 21, are in Aramaic. The words, in Matthew, are more nearly Hebrew: he writes *Helei*: it is easier to see that this could have been taken for a cry to Elias (Eli-jah) than Mark's *Eloi*. But (1) all save the first syllable may have been lost: or (2) the cry was *not* taken for a call to Elias, but such Jews as remembered that Elias was to come to extricate the Messias from an obscure life of poverty will have made a cruel jest—and pretended that it was to Elias that Jesus was calling. It is true that our Lord must have been experiencing a sense of complete desolation and that His sensitive human nature must have been as it were shut off from the action of His divine nature: but if our Lord used the first verse of that Psalm He cannot have forgotten the rest of it—even we, if we know it well, can hardly do so. And while the Psalm begins with a terrible cry of desolation, it gradually changes into a declaration that God will not forsake the sufferer and has not forsaken him, but will glorify him, and that his triumph will be known to all—yes, and to generations yet unborn.

36. This must have been one of the soldiers; they always took flasks of thin wine (*posca*) with them, and these had often a sponge stuffed into the neck as 'stopper'. He put this on to a

37. And Jesus, having cried out with a loud voice, gave up the ghost.

The Rending of the Veil: *the Centurion*: *the Holy Women*: 38–41
(Matt. 27: 51–56; Luke 23: 45b, 47–49; John 19: 31–37)

38. And the veil of the temple was rent in two, from the top to the bottom.

39. And the centurion who stood over against him, seeing that crying

---

reed or cane, and lifted it to our Lord's lips. (St John (19: 29) says he put it on a 'hyssop', but that soft-stemmed plant could not have supported a sponge soaked in wine or anything else. There is reason to suppose that St John wrote 'hyssos', a short javelin, and to one watching from a distance, as presumably Peter did, this will have looked like a cane or any other sort of rod.) One would say that people tried to stop the soldier: 'Let me alone', he said: 'let us see if Elias will come and take him down!' We may judge that he was a kind-hearted man, and that, touched by our Lord's desperate cry, he ran up with the wine, and was checked by the mockers, who knew enough Latin to explain that our Lord was calling for Elias. If we could take 'saying' as a plural participle (as it is in some MSS. which read λέγοντες for λέγων), it would be simple: it would have been the *others* who said: 'Stop! let us see, etc.', and this is indeed nearer to Matthew.

37. St Mark leaves the 'loud cry' inarticulate: see Luke 23: 46 and John 19: 30 for our Lord's last 'words' on the Cross.

38. There were two veils in the temple, one hanging over the entrance to the ἱερόν or 'Holy Place'; the other, over the door into the 'Holy of Holies'. Probably the exterior veil is meant, for the prodigy must have been visible to all (cf. Hebr. 9: 3, 9; 10: 19). The old Dispensation was finished with: there was now no more veil separating man from God. Notice that the veil was torn from the top downwards, as though emphasizing divine action: human hands could not have reached the top to tear it.

out in this manner he had given up the ghost, said: Indeed this man was the son of God.

40. And there were also women looking on afar off: among whom was Mary Magdalen and Mary the mother of James the Less and of Joseph and Salome.

41. Who also when he was in Galilee followed him and ministered to him, and many other women that came up with him to Jerusalem.

The Burial: 42–47

(Matt. 27: 57–61; Luke 23: 50–55; John 19: 38–42)

42. And when evening was now come (because it was the Parasceve, that is, the day before the sabbath),

---

39. 'Crying out' ($\kappa\rho\acute{a}\xi as$); is sometimes omitted after 'in this manner': the centurion (a Latin word used by St Mark for $\acute{\epsilon}\kappa a\tau\acute{o}\nu\tau a\rho\chi os$ in Matthew and Luke) saw that Jesus had died thus, very soon, and with a strong cry instead of slowly weakening, felt that there was something superhuman here, and exclaimed that 'Truly—this man was a son of God', which on pagan lips will not have meant more than 'divine' in a wide sense, and indeed St Luke says 'righteous' only.

40, 41. Mary of Magdala (Luke 8: 2). Mary, mother of James 'the little' (it can mean the 'younger') and (as before) Joseph is mentioned again in verse 47. Salome was probably mother of the sons of Zebedee (see Matt. 20: 20; 27: 56).

42. Usually 'evening' ($\acute{o}\psi\acute{\iota}a$) means a fairly late hour; but since the Pasch began about 6 p.m., Joseph's hurried coming and going must have taken place between 3 p.m. and 6. Since it was only the 'preparation', i.e. the day before the Sabbath (the actual Pasch), all this activity and purchasing could still take place. Roman custom involved dead bodies remaining on their cross; but Jewish law (Deut. 21: 23) demanded that they should be buried the same day. Roman law permitted the dead to be handed over on request from relatives, though the petition was not always granted, e.g. if the victim had

43. Joseph of Arimathea, a noble counsellor, who was also himself looking for the kingdom of God, came and went in boldly to Pilate and begged the body of Jesus.

44. But Pilate wondered that he should be already dead. And sending for the centurion, he asked him if he were already dead.

45. And when he had understood it by the centurion, he gave the body to Joseph.

46. And Joseph, buying fine linen and taking him down, wrapped him up in the fine linen and laid him in a sepulchre which was hewed out of a rock. And he rolled a stone to the door of the sepulchre.

47. And Mary Magdalen and Mary the mother of Joseph, beheld where he was laid.

---

been guilty of treason. The custom, if not law, dated back to Augustus; Joseph therefore knew that he had this on his side. Arimathea may be a town in Judea, between Bethlehem and Hebron.

43. Joseph was a member of the Sanhedrin, which shows that even that assembly had not been unanimous. 'Noble' ($\epsilon\upsilon\sigma\chi\eta\mu\omega\nu$) should mean 'handsome' but had come to mean wealthy, or at least distinguished. It took some courage to approach the Procurator who had been disgusted by the whole proceeding: but Pilate, while surprised by so rapid a death, had

45. the facts vouched for by the centurion (this is only in Mark) and 'granted' ($\epsilon\delta\omega\rho\eta\sigma\alpha\tau o$) the body to Joseph.

46. He therefore bought a *sindon* a length of fine linen in which he wrapped the body: St Mark, brief as he is, feels compelled to say, vividly, that the grave was a rock-grave: the entrance was comparatively small: it was entirely blocked by a round stone that was rolled along a groove and could be rolled to and fro ($\pi\rho o\varsigma$- and $\alpha\pi o$-$\kappa\upsilon\lambda\iota\epsilon\iota\nu$).

47. Only two women are mentioned, and Joseph appears no more save in legends, e.g. those concerned with Glastonbury and the Grail.

CHAPTER SIXTEEN

The Women find the Sepulchre Empty: 1–8

(Matt. 28: 1–8; Luke 24: 1–10; cf. John 20: 1 ff.)

1. And when the sabbath was past, Mary Magdalen and Mary the mother of James and Salome, brought sweet spices, that coming, they might anoint Jesus.
2. And very early in the morning, the first day of the week, they come to the sepulchre, the sun being now risen.
3. And they said one to another: Who shall roll us back the stone from the door of the sepulchre?
4. And looking, they saw the stone rolled back. For it was very great.

---

1. They had bought (not 'brought') perfumed oils as well as aromatic herbs.
2. 'The first day of the week' (μία τῶν σαββάτων) must mean 'one day *from* the Sabbath', or 'the first day of the week following the Sabbath', for the paschal feast lasted a week, though work was started again when the 'great sabbath' was over. Dawn and dusk are very brief in that latitude—in April the sun rises about six—so, since St Mark will not have contradicted himself within one line, we assume that 'very early' means from the point of view of starting on their enterprise: when they arrived in the garden the sun had risen. They did not, presumably, all live in the same house: it took time to assemble their little company and to make sure of what spices, etc., they had ready: St John (20: 1) says that when Mary Magdalen came to the tomb, it was still dark.
4. 'For', γάρ, is quite in St Mark's style; he likes to explain afterwards something he has just said: 'they were anxious,

169

5. And entering into the sepulchre, they saw a young man sitting on the right side, clothed with a white robe: and they were astonished.
6. Who saith to them: Be not affrighted. You seek Jesus of Nazareth, who was crucified. He is risen: he is not here. Behold the place where they laid him.
7. But go, tell his disciples and Peter that he goeth before you into Galilee. There you shall see him, as he told you.
8. But they going out, fled from the sepulchre: for a trembling and fear had seized them. And they said nothing to any man: for they were afraid.

Appendix (i): 9-11

(John 20: 11-18)

9. But he rising early the first day of the week, appeared first to Mary Magdalen, out of whom he had cast seven devils.

---

for . . .' In a rock tomb, there might be a stone 'bench' at the back and on either side, or only one at the back. Since the angel was 'seated' on the right, it seems that there were at least two such 'benches': the angel will hardly have placed himself just where our Lord's body had lain, and afterwards we find that the grave-clothes were visible and undisturbed.
6. 'Astonished' ($\dot{\epsilon}\kappa\theta\alpha\mu\beta\epsilon\hat{\imath}\sigma\theta\epsilon$) is more than to be frightened: they were almost stupefied by the empty tomb, the angelic apparition. Not 'who was crucified', but, 'the Crucified'; it is almost a 'surname': cf. 1 Cor. 1: 23; 2: 2; Gal. 2: 1. 'He rose', '$\dot{\eta}\gamma\dot{\epsilon}\rho\theta\eta$: the aorist points to a past moment: St Paul can contemplate our Lord not only as 'the Crucified', but as permanently risen and alive (the perfect: 1 Cor. 15: 4, 20).
7. 'Do not stop here—*but* go, etc.' Peter is singled out, either as chief of the apostles, or as needing special encouragement. St Mark tells us nothing about the appearances in Jerusalem and indeed suggests that there were not to be any. Our Lord may have hastened His appearances out of compassion for the sorrowful and bewildered apostles.
8. The women had recovered sufficiently to run away but were

10. She went and told them that had been with him, who were mourning and weeping.
11. And they hearing that he was alive and had been seen by her, did not believe.

Appendix (ii): 12, 13

(Luke 24: 13–32)

12. And after that he appeared in another shape to two of them walking, as they were going into the country.
13. And they going told it to the rest: neither did they believe them.

---

still terrified and said nothing to anyone (see note at the end of this chapter.)

9. Mary Magdalen is 'defined' as though she had not yet been mentioned: cf. Luke 8: 2. St Paul (1 Cor. 15: 5) does not allude to any of the apparitions to the holy women (they were not, like the apostles, *official* witnesses), and puts Peter as seeing our Lord before the other apostles saw Him, not implying that no one saw Him previously: instinctively, Catholics feel that He will first of all have made our Lady aware of His resurrection.
10. 'She' (ἐκείνη) as subject occurs only twice, so far, in Mark, but thrice in this concluding section: 'went' (πορεύεσθαι) is a colourless word and not used elsewhere by St Mark (9: 30 is very doubtful; but the word too comes thrice in this section, though about 30 times in Matthew, and about 50 in Luke). She said He was alive and she had *seen* Him, but they did not believe.
11. Luke). She said He was alive and she had *seen* Him, but they did not believe.
12, 13. Thus curtly does the author relate what St Luke tells so fully and movingly. Even though St Luke 24: 35) says that the apostles declared that the Lord was risen and had appeared to Peter, it is psychologically understandable that *still* a doubt lurked in their minds, till they too, themselves, should have 'seen'.

Appendix (iii): 14

(Luke 24: 36 ff.; John 20: 19 ff.; Matt. 28 ff. Cf. 1 Cor. 15: 5)

14. At length he appeared to the eleven as they were at table: and he upbraided them with their incredulity and hardness of heart, because they did not believe them who had seen him after he was risen again.

Appendix (iv): 15–18

15. And he said to them: Go ye into the whole world and preach the gospel to every creature.

16. He that believeth and is baptized shall be saved: but he that believeth not shall be condemned.

17. And these signs shall follow them that believe: In my name they shall cast out devils. They shall speak with new tongues.

---

14. We think that this apparition took place on the Sunday: but from now on, the author 'telescopes' the life of the Risen Christ and mentions neither places nor times. The word 'at length', ὕστερον, means 'finally' only in regard of the apparitions mentioned so far; it would in no case suit the Galilean apparitions, for by then the apostles had often seen our Lord, and *had* believed. But, the word is not in St Mark's vocabulary: each time that St Matthew says ὕστερον (22: 27; 21: 37), St Mark writes ἔσχατον.

15. 'Creature' (κτίσις) in Mark (10: 6; 13: 19) means the creative act: here, creatures: it occurs in this sense often in St Paul, e.g. Rom. 8: 19, 20, 21, 22.

16. The fact of believing implies obedience to the laws laid down by Christ: 'he that believeth not', ἀπιστεῖν, to refuse one's belief renders any question of baptism evidently idle.

17, 18. The Church always possesses the gift of miracles: in proportion as the Faith becomes known, exterior 'signs' are less necessary and indeed spiritual, interior miracles are in themselves more valuable. To work miracles is not granted to each and every Christian; but the march of the Faith is always accompanied by sufficient 'signs'.

18. They shall take up serpents: and if they shall drink any deadly thing, it shall not hurt them. They shall lay their hands upon the sick: and they shall recover.

Appendix (v): 19, 20

(Cf. Luke 24: 50 ff.; Acts 1: 9; 1 Peter 3: 22; Romans 8: 34; Hebr. 8: 1)

19. And the Lord Jesus, after he had spoken to them, was taken up into heaven and sitteth on the right hand of God.
20. But they going forth preached everywhere: the Lord working withal, and confirming the word with signs that followed.

---

19. 'The Lord Jesus' is not found in the gospels save in Luke 24: 3 and often in the Acts. Given the 'skeleton outline' thus provided by the author, it cannot be said that 'after speaking to them' certainly refers to what was said at Jerusalem in the days following the resurrection: still less does the author assert that the ascension took place on Easter Sunday. Ἀνελήφθη 'was taken up', like Elias (4 Kings 2: 11): this expresses the will of the Father that His Son should be glorified: other words, 'to go up, proceed up, to heaven' (ἀναβῆναι, πυρευθῆναι εἰς οὐρανόν) imply our Lord's inherent power: e.g. John 6: 62; 20: 17: (1 Pet. 3: 22; Hebr. 4: 14). In the East, our feast of the Ascension is still called 'taking up', (ἀναληψις): we distinguish carefully between the Ascension and our Lady's Assumption.

Note on 16: 9–20

We must explain the problem set by these verses, in the fewest possible words, recalling that the 'Biblical Commission' has said we may not *affirm* that these verses are not inspired or canonical; and that it is not *demonstrated* (proved) that they are not by St Mark.

1. Various MSS., among them the very important fourth-century Vatican and Sinaitic MSS. (Greek) altogether lack these verses, though the Vatican MS. leaves a column and a half blank into which verses 9–20 *could* have been compressed.

A certain number of MSS. have a very short version of the canonical ending which always (save once) is added as well as the longer. This shorter ending can be disregarded, for it was accepted by a very few and serves only to show that (as we know) there were MSS. which lacked the canonical ending, and, that the writer either did not know or it or disapproved of it. Enough, now, to say that all the other versions, especially the Latin, contain the verses as in our 'Gospel'. As for the Fathers of the Church, many of the most important, e.g. Tertullian, SS. Cyprian, Athanasius, Cyril of Jerusalem, seem unaware of the longer ending, but this is merely 'negative' witness *unless* they are writing about baptism, when you would expect them to have quoted it. St Jerome (who maintains it) says it is lacking in nearly all the Greek MSS.; and Eusebius (c. 300) is in reality hostile to it but refrains from positively rejecting it. However, older witnesses, e.g. SS. Justin (c. 120) and Irenaeus (c. 130) quote it; so do the two oldest Syrian writers.

2. From the literary point of view, it does not follow that the author of a book writes all of it, or finishes it, himself: thus assuming that *Deuteronomy* was written substantially by Moses, we cannot suppose that he finished it with an account of his own death. It has been suggested that the last page of St Mark's MS. may have been torn off, accidentally or on purpose (as apparently in contradiction with Luke about the time of the Resurrection). But not only is this supposition arbitrary, but the accident would have had to happen to the very first MS. (the 'archetype') and we would have to assume that only a truncated edition of Mark was circulated till an unknown hand added a 'conclusion'. We think that St Mark *did* stop writing at verse 8; but that verse, as an 'ending', is so extremely abrupt that we may feel it probable that he intended to write more but for some reason was prevented from doing so immediately. St Luke ends his gospel hardly less abruptly, but did intend to write a second treatise and in fact wrote one—the Acts. We think, then,

that the actual ending is either by St Mark, a mere draft of
what he proposed to write later or, was added by another.
It is in fact clear that there is a break between verses 8 and 9.
The story starts again with the resurrection and Mary
Magdalen is introduced and 'defined' as she from whom the
Lord cast out seven devils, though she was mentioned only a
few verses earlier. The section is but a dry résumé and very
unlike the vivacity of St Mark, terse though he be. It is true
that his favourite word εὐθύς would have had no sufficient
reason for appearing in this 'ending', but πάλιν would:
anyhow neither of them does: and words that appear only
here, φαίνεσθαι, θεᾶσθαι, ἀπιστεῖν need not have been
used in the earlier chapters, though they quite reasonably
might have been. On the whole, then, we may think that
the ending was a résumé added by St Mark himself till he
could write something more satisfactory, or, more probably,
by another. We cannot think that a solitary Armenian MS.,
A.D. 986, introducing the final verses with the words 'by the
presbyter Aristion' can prove that Aristion in fact wrote them,
though Eusebius does say that an Aristion was mentioned by
Papias as a disciple of our Lord's, and parts of whose com-
mentaries on the words of Christ he quotes; but he says
nothing to connect him with St Mark. Clement of Alexandria
suggests St Peter did not wholly approve of St Mark's
document; so he may have told him to tear off the end of it
and various tentative endings may have been experimented
with. But this is only speculative, and while it seems clear
that St Mark did not really mean his 'gospel' to end at verse
8, there is no proof whether it was he or another who very
soon added the verses that now form the canonical ending.

QUESTIONS

1. Why is it commonly held that St Mark in his gospel wrote down the recollections of St Peter?
2. What does this gospel tell us about St Peter?
3. What evidence is there in this gospel that Mark was writing for gentile readers?
4. What incidents or sayings from this gospel show the impression made by Jesus on the twelve disciples and their attitude towards Him?
5. Give some account of our Lord's relations with His enemies.
6. What do we learn in this gospel about John the Baptist?
7. Give an outline of the events of the Galilean ministry.
8. Describe and explain the healing of the man with the palsy.
9. Explain the parables about the children of the wedding feast, the patched garments and the new wine in old bottles.
10. Give an account of some events in this gospel which took place on the Sabbath.
11. What is the teaching in the parables about the Kingdom of God?
12. Describe *one* occasion in this gospel on which our Lord cured someone suffering from diabolical possession.
13. Describe how Jairus's daughter was brought back to life.
14. Give some account of the training of the Twelve Apostles.
15. Describe the Feeding of the Five Thousand.
16. What is the 'tradition of the ancients'? Give an account of our Lord's words on this subject.
17. Describe the circumstances of Peter's recognition at Caesarea Philippi of our Lord as the Christ.
18. Describe the Transfiguration. Relate our Lord's teaching which directly followed it.

19. 'Grant to us that we may sit, one on thy right hand and the other on thy left hand.' Relate the events which led to this request, and the teaching that our Lord gave as a result of it.

20. Describe the events of Palm Sunday, and of the rest of Holy Week until the beginning of Maundy Thursday.

21. Tell the story of and explain what happened on 'The Day of Questions'.

22. Relate and explain the parable of the Wicked Husbandmen.

23. Give an account of our Lord's teaching about the fall of Jerusalem and the end of the world.

24. What does the gospel tell us about the Last Supper, the preparation for it and the events which happened at it?

25. Describe our Lord's trial before the Sanhedrin.

26. Relate the events which occurred during our Lord's trial before Pilate.

27. Describe the course of our Lord's Passion from the end of His trial before Pilate until His burial in the tomb.

28. What account does St Mark give of the Resurrection and of Christ's appearances afterwards?

29. Give an account of our Lord's teaching on the following: the Kingdom, Faith, Taking up the Cross, Humility, Scandal, Marriage, Riches, Prayer, the Need to Watch.

30. Write notes on: the Synagogue, the Sabbath, the Temple, the Pasch, the High Priest, the Sadducees, the Pharisees, the sons of Zebedee, Capharnaum, Levi, loaves of proposition, Idumea, Tyre and Sidon, Beelzebub, the brethren of Christ, the Gerasenes, Jairus, Herod, Herodias, Bethsaida, Gennesareth, Corban, Decapolis, Ephpheta, Dalmanutha, Caesarea Philippi, Elias, Jericho, Bartimaeus, Bethany, Herod's party, the Scribes, the Temple treasury, Gethsemani, Simon of Cyrene, Mary Magdalen, Mary the mother of James and Joseph, Salome, Joseph of Arimathea, the publicans, the barren fig tree.